RESOURCE BOOKS FOR TEACHERS

series editor

ALAN MALEY

TRANSLATION

Alan Duff

Oxford University Press 1989

Oxford University Press
Walton Street, Oxford OX2 6DP

Oxford   New York   Toronto
Delhi   Bombay   Calcutta   Madras   Karachi
Petaling Jaya   Singapore   Hong Kong   Tokyo
Nairobi   Dar es Salaam   Cape Town
Melbourne   Auckland

and associated companies in
Berlin   Ibadan

Oxford, Oxford English and the *Oxford English logo* are trade marks of
Oxford University Press

ISBN 0 19 437104 2

Set by Pentacor Ltd, High Wycombe, Bucks

Printed in Hong Kong

Acknowledgements

To all the following my sincere thanks for help, encouragement, and welcome advice:

Mary and Tim Bowen, Marija Cvelić (Ekonomski Fakultet, Split), Patricia Downey, Sukla Mitra (British Council, Calcutta), Peter Newmark, Sue O'Connell, Momir Pejović (and colleagues at *Sterijino Pozorje*, Novi Sad), Mario Rinvolucri, Lyn Robertson (British Council, Belgrade), Dr Tibor Várady, Catherine Walter, and Bob Wilkinson (Rijkshogeschool, Maastricht).

A word of special gratitude to my wife Márta for her patience and ever practical help, and to Roger Neal for his kindness and generous hospitality.

The publisher would like to thank the following for their permission to use copyright material:

Air France (for an extract from 'Le Musée de l'assistance publique des Hôpitaux de Paris' in *Atlas*); *The Architectural Review* (for 'Proposals for Restructing Kuwait'); BBC Bristol (for the letter to the Residents of Windsor Terrace and Windsor Place); Jonathan Cape and Equinox (for a number of extracts from *Manwatching*, by Desmond Morris); Curtis Brown and André Deutsch (for 'The Purist', by Ogden Nash); André Deutsch (for an extract from *How to be an Alien*, by George Mikes); Mrs Valerie Eliot and Faber and Faber (for a letter reproduced in *The Times*); Faber and Faber, and Peters, Fraser, and Dunlop (for two extracts from *Look Back in Anger*, by John Osborne); Frederick Fuller (for an interview on translation); *The Guardian* (for 'Remedies', and an extract from the obituary of Trevor Howard); *The Listener* (for short extracts from articles and from an interview between Melvyn Bragg and Len Deighton); Lutterworth Press (for a passage from *Journeys to the Past*, by David Attenborough); *New Scientist* (for part of an article on Immunotoxins and for other short extracts) *The Observer* (for 'Britain falls foul of water clean-up bid'); Penguin Books (for a number of excerpts from *Fundamentals of Psychology*, by C. J. Adcock, and various extracts from *The Psychology of Perception*, by M. D. Vernon); Peters, Fraser, and Dunlop (for an extract from 'Every one a wincer', by Philip Norman, in *The Times*); Phaidon Press (for material from 'Visual Metaphors of Value in Art' in *Meditations on a Hobby Horse*, by E. H. Gombrich); *The Sunday Times* (for an extract from 'Wildlife driven to the wall in the Kalahari', by Brian Jackman and Peter Godwin); *The Times* (for part of the 'Letter from Timbuktu', by Paul Vallely, excerpts from 'Proving Einstein Wrong', by Robert Matthews, 'Humbug behind the headlines', by T. E. Utley, and 'Laughing back at life', by Chris Peachment); and Unwin Hyman and Rand McNally (for an extract from *Aku-Aku*, by Thor Heyerdahl).

The publisher would also like to thank the following for their permission to use appeal and publicity material, and to reproduce artwork:
Canadian High Commission
Cancer Relief Macmillan Fund
Epson Computers
Musicians Benevolent Fund
Pilkington Glass
Private Eye
RAC
United Distillers
Whitbread Co PLC

Illustrations by:
Ffolkes
Ken Pyne
Axel Scheffler

To Michael Swan, poet and friend

Contents

The author and series editor		1
Foreword		3
Introduction		5
How to use this book		13

1 Context and register   19

Activity   *Focus*

1.1	Context clues	Suggesting likely sources for fragments of language	22
1.2	Matching pairs	Passages divided into two parts: suggesting a context for the language, and predicting the content of the missing half	25
1.3	Implications	The use of inverted commas; the difference between stated meaning and implied meaning	28
1.4	Alternatives	Choice of words: alternative wordings	30
1.5	Transformations	Exercises in register: statements transformed to suit different levels of formality	37
1.6	Odd man out	Groups of words or expressions, one of which does not properly belong	39
1.7	Colloquial expressions	Common colloquial expressions; emphasis on adjectival expressions and phrasal verbs	42
1.8	Word play	Ambiguous or oddly-worded statements	47

2 Word order and reference   49

2.1	Stress and emphasis	Stress on particular words, marked or implied by the writer/speaker	50
2.2	Word order: opening words	Inversion of normal word order	54
2.3	Reformulation and repetition	Saying the same thing in different words or repeating words already used	57
2.4	Articles	The use of *a, the, one,* and *its* in English and L1	60
2.5	Compounds	Expressions which allow for compression of thought	63

2.6	Reference and meaning	Referential words (*which, that, it, what, this*)	66
2.7	Short cuts: contractions and substitutes	Uncompleted structures, half sentences, missing words; emphatic use of *did, was,* and *is*	70

3 Time: tense, mood, and aspect — 73

3.1	The *-ing, -ed,* and *-en* forms	Words ending in *-ing, -ed, -en*	74
3.2	Passive forms	Use of the passive in English	78
3.3	Conditionals	Focus on possibility: the function of *if, were, had, would, could, might*	86
3.4	Time: tenses, adverbs, and prepositions	The function of *still, since, by, then, now, before, ago, while,* and *during*	92

4 Concepts and notions — 97

4.1	Choice of words: Call my bluff	A word game based on definitions, real and imaginary	99
4.2	Choice of words: definitions and distinctions	The meaning of specific expressions and of close synonyms	102
4.3	Choice of words: word play	Brief definitions for translation	107
4.4	Possibility and ability	The concept of *can* or *be able,* and *opportunity, potential, chance, ability,* etc.	109
4.5	Causality: consequence, effect, and result	Language associated with *cause* and how things are made to occur	112
4.6	Perception: seeing and understanding	Language associated with *seeing* (vision and perception)	117

5 Idiom: from one culture to another — 123

5.1	The translator and the text: defective and ambiguous sentences	Discussion of faulty sentences in English	125
5.2	The translator and the text: choice of words	Discussion of texts translated into English	128
5.3	On the beaten track: familiar expressions	Formula language and fixed expressions (cliché, jargon, standard metaphor)	133
5.4	Colloquialisms	Colloquial language, proverbs, and common sayings	136
5.5	Variations on a theme: reformulations	Different versions of the same text	144

5.6 Variations on a theme: reverse translation   Identifying how errors occur through two-way translations   147

5.7 Spoken language, written language: voices of the past   Writing from previous centuries   149

5.8 Spoken language, written language: speech in writing   Working on transcriptions from interviews and radio talks   152

5.9 Spoken language, written language: translation and adaptation; subtitles and synchronization   Adapting texts for newspapers, television, and radio   154

Annotated bibliography   158

The author and series editor

Alan Duff has been a lecturer at Novi Sad University and an Assistant English Language Officer for The British Council. He has also spent a year touring India for The British Council, giving lectures on language, literature, and translation. Most recently he taught for three months at the University of Shijiazhuang, People's Republic of China. For the past fifteen years he has also worked as a freelance writer/translator, specializing in drama, literature, and television work.

In addition to the books he has co-authored with Alan Maley (see below), he has also written *That's Life!* and *The Third Language* (on translation into English).

As a translator, he has published over 30 stage plays and films. He has also published several novels, short stories, and historical works.

Alan Maley worked for The British Council from 1962–1988, serving as English Language Officer in Yugoslavia, Ghana, Italy, France, and China, and as Regional Representative for The British Council in South India (Madras). He is currently Director-General of the Bell Educational Trust, Cambridge.

He wrote *Quartet* (with Françoise Grellet and Wim Welsing, OUP 1982). He has also written *Beyond Words, Sounds Interesting, Sounds Intriguing, Words, Variations on a Theme,* and *Drama Techniques in Language Learning* (all with Alan Duff), *The Mind's Eye* (with Françoise Grellet and Alan Duff), and *Learning to Listen* and *Poem into Poem* (with Sandra Moulding). He is also Series Editor for the Oxford Supplementary Skills Series.

Foreword

Translation has long languished as a poor relation in the family of language teaching techniques. It has been denigrated as 'uncommunicative', 'boring', 'pointless', 'difficult', 'irrelevant', and the like, and has suffered from too close an association with its cousin, Grammar. Along with its other traditional cousins Literature, Dictation, Vocabulary, Reading Aloud, etc., it has been pushed into the methodological lumber room.

Only recently, as the communicative movement has begun to run short of ideas, has there been a resurgence of interest in traditional practices such as translation. Could it be that it serves some useful purpose after all? Could it be renovated, reinterpreted, humanized, made communicative?

Judging by the activities in Alan Duff's book, the answer has to be 'yes'. Its great originality lies in having successfully shifted the emphasis from *learning* translation as a set of discrete skills to *using* translation as a resource for the promotion of language learning. To quote from the Introduction 'Translation develops three qualities essential to all language learning: accuracy, clarity, and flexibility. It trains the reader to search (flexibility) for the most appropriate words (accuracy) to convey what is meant (clarity).'

The activities are designed to develop these three qualities. Many of the activities can be used to develop language awareness, without necessarily proceeding to the final stage of translation at all. This will therefore be a book of value to those who wish to refine their students' sensitivity to alternative ways of expressing meaning, as well as to those who wish to train their students to apply this sensitivity to rendering English texts into their own language.

'Awareness raising' has become a piece of facile jargon. However, few teachers or students who work through the activities in this book can fail to have their awareness of language heightened, and their perceptions changed.

Alan Maley

Introduction

Why translation?

> Translation, as the process of conveying messages across linguistic and cultural barriers, is an eminently communicative activity, one whose use could well be considered in a wider range of teaching situations than may currently be the case.
>
> (Dr Ian Tudor)

For the past two decades or more, translation has been generally out of favour with the language teaching community. (Almost, we might say, 'sent to Siberia'!) Yet for thousands of years this ancient craft had been right at the heart of language learning. Indeed, of almost all learning, for many of the mediaeval universities developed out of what were originally schools of translation.

Yet today translation is largely ignored as a valid activity for language practice and improvement. And even where it is still retained, it tends to be used not for language teaching, but for testing.

The main reason for this, I think, is that over the centuries translation had gradually become fossilized. It became less and less associated with the excitement of new discoveries, more and more with the tedium of book learning. What should have been a vital and challenging discipline had degenerated in most schools into a pointless routine exercise, a chore, and a punishment.

If translation has fallen from favour in our times, it is largely because teachers feel, with some justification, that:

a. it is text-bound, and confined to only two skills – reading and writing; it is not a communicative activity because it involves no oral interaction
b. it is not suitable for classroom work because the students must do the writing on their own; it is also time-consuming and wasteful
c. it is associated with 'different language', with literary or scientific texts, and is not suited to the general needs of the language learner.

> The widespread use of literary-type texts for translation seems to us both an anachronistic and a wasteful activity if the wider objective of work in translation is deemed to be one of informing *all other areas* of the learners' communicative repertoire.
>
> (A. G. Weymouth, my italics)

d. use of the mother tongue is required, and this is not desirable
e. and, finally, it is boring – both to do, and to correct.

This may be the case, but it need not be so. Translation does not have to be a lone, pointless struggle between student and text. Many other approaches are possible. Translation can be introduced, purposefully and imaginatively, into the language learning programme. There, I believe, it deserves its place – along with other approaches – for the reasons that follow.

Reasons for using translation in the classroom

1 Influence of the mother tongue

We all have a mother tongue, or first language. This shapes our way of thinking, and to some extent our use of the foreign language (pronunciation, choice of words, tone, word order, etc.). Translation helps us to understand better the influence of the one language on the other, and to correct errors of habit that creep in unnoticed (such as the misuse of particular words or structures). And, because translation involves contrast, it enables us to explore the potential of both languages – their strengths and weaknesses.

2 Naturalness of the activity

Translation is a natural and necessary activity. More so, indeed, than many of the fashionable activities invented for language learners. Outside the classroom – in offices, banks, factories, shops, and airports – translation is going on all the time. Why not inside the classroom?

3 The skills aspect

Language competence is a two-way, not a one-way system. We need to be able to communicate both ways: into and from the foreign language. Textbooks, understandably, place great emphasis on competence in the foreign language. Yet little guidance is given on how to communicate back into the mother tongue, as many professionals need to do in their daily work. Translation is ideally suited for practising this vital skill.

4 The reality of language

The proper material of translation is authentic, not 'made up' language. And all language is relevant to translation – all styles and registers of both speech and writing. Translation need not be confined to literature!

Because the material is authentic and wide-ranging in scope, the learner is being brought into touch with the whole language, and not just those parts isolated by the textbook. This is an aim to be found in almost all course descriptions: 'to increase the students' power and range of expression'. Translation will certainly do this.

5 Usefulness

As a language learning activity, translation has many merits. Chief among these are:

a. It is an activity which, by its very nature, invites speculation and discussion. In translation, there is rarely a 'right' answer (though there may be several wrong ones!). It is not necessary for all the work in class to be done alone and in writing. Students can work in groups for oral discussion. The texts, which can be very short, serve as material both for reading and for discussion.

b. Translation develops three qualities essential to all language learning: accuracy, clarity, and flexibility. It trains the learner to search (flexibility) for the most appropriate words (accuracy) to convey what is meant (clarity). This combination of freedom and constraint allows the students to contribute their own thoughts to a discussion which has a clear focus – the text.

c. Depending on the students' needs, and on the syllabus, the teacher can select material to illustrate particular aspects of language and structure with which the students have difficulty in English (for instance, prepositions, articles, *if*-clauses, the passive). By working through these difficulties in the mother tongue, the students come to see the link between language (grammar) and usage. An example of this is the use of the passive in signs and notices (PARKING PROHIBITED, NO CREDIT ALLOWED) in English. In another language these might be rendered differently (Do not Park Here, We Give No Credit).

d. Translators will always be needed. Without them, there would be no summit talks, no *glasnost* or *perestroika*, no Cannes Film Festival, no Nobel prizes, no advances in medicine, science, or engineering, no international law, no Olympic Games, no *Hamlet*, no *War and Peace* . . .

And who is to do all this necessary work? Either the professionals themselves, or the students of language. Only translation can give them the training they need.

Rationale of the book

It must be stressed that this book is not a training manual for professional translators (though they could certainly use it). Nor is it a coursebook on how to teach translation (though plenty of advice is offered). *Translation* is a resource book for teachers who wish to use *translation* as a language learning activity, just as they might use *literature, drama, project work, conversation, role play, writing,* or *class readers* for language practice and improvement.

The aim of *Translation* is to provide the teacher with source material (in English) which reflects most characteristic features of the language (-*ing* forms, compounds, *if*-clauses, articles, etc.); which gives students practice in translating a variety of styles and registers (colloquial, formal, and idiomatic usages); which provides a basis for writing and discussion; and which is suitable for use with the many different translation techniques suggested.

1 Practice

Students of language are often required to translate, but they are rarely given any practice in the skill. Textbooks and examination papers toss at them questions beginning: 'Translate the following sentences into Gujarati/French/Hungarian/Dutch . . .' But the sentences are often made up, or the texts chosen specifically for their 'language traps'. This is an abuse of translation.

One of the aims of this book is to suggest that there is no point in merely handing out texts to the students once a week with the instruction: 'Translate!' This is a random approach which serves little purpose.

Practice in translation does not mean setting written assignments to be returned to the students with the errors marked in red. It means, rather, giving the students regular opportunities to compare and discuss their work with others, and to respond to suggestions.

2 Purpose

Translation takes time, care, and thought. A student who has to spend an hour, maybe two hours, struggling over a text may want to ask: 'Why am I doing this? Could not the time be better spent?'

If the teacher cannot explain why the activity is being done – and this holds for all kinds of language activity – the student is likely to feel frustrated.

This is why I have grouped the activities in *Translation* under headings which should give the teacher a clear, if general, idea of the language focus (for example, *word order, stress, compounds, passive forms,* etc.).

Students are often asked to translate without being given any introduction to the kind of material they will be working on. As a result, they are not mentally prepared for the activity. This is a weakness I wished to avoid. Hence the importance given in the book to the *warm-up* activities. These are generally oral tasks designed to set the students thinking along specific lines. So, for instance, before working on texts which focus on the translation of articles, they first suggest titles of songs, books, or films in English, and offer oral translations.

3 Time

One of the strongest objections to the use of translation is that it is time-consuming and 'wasteful'. And, indeed, it often is. There is little point in asking 20 or 30 people to sit silently in a room translating the same text. They might just as well do the work at home.

In order to avoid this wastage, and to make best use of the students' time, I have followed certain basic principles in devising the activities:

a. all students should be equally involved in the task; nobody should be kept 'hanging around'
b. the activities should involve as much oral translation as possible; the writing can often be done in the form of notes, to be used in later discussion
c. the material itself should preferably be short and varied (longer texts being reserved mainly for out-of-class work)
d. time-limits should be set, where necessary, in order to prevent the students from getting 'stuck', and to ensure that sufficient time is left for discussion.

This does not mean, however, that the students should be hurried, or encouraged to make hasty decisions. To prevent this happening, I have designed the task sheets (of passages for translation) in such a way that the students work only on a little material at a time. This also helps to keep their interest alive, as it allows for the circulation of fresh material. In all the activities, I have tried to strike a balance between giving the students too much time to think, and too little. Translation constantly involves making choices. The longer you sit on the fence, the harder it is to make up your mind. Often the best solutions occur to us after the thinking has been done and a choice made. The function of the discussion, then, is to give the students time for further reflection, and a chance to change their minds.

4 Material

Since this book was designed to be used by language teachers all over the world, it was important, I felt, that the material should satisfy the two requirements implicit in the title *Translation*. Firstly, it should illustrate the most common basic principles, problems, challenges, and strategies of translation in general. Secondly, it should provide the teacher with material directly relevant to the study of English and, in particular, to language practice through the medium of translation *from* English.

In order to avoid confusion, and to keep the fundamental concept of the book clear, I have not entered into speculation about the problems of translating from other languages into English. That is a separate matter. The bedrock of this book is English.

In selecting the material, the thought which was uppermost in my mind was this: If I were a language teacher working with students whose mother tongue was not English, what kind of book would I want? Surely, one which would offer me a wide range of material which would reliably reflect those aspects of English (compounds, -*ing* forms) which are most characteristic of the language, and also challenging to translate? Other principles which influenced my choice were:

a. the material should represent customary usage in both written and spoken language; it should cover the full range of styles and registers (from highly formal to colloquial)
b. in content, it should be general rather than specialized, so that it could be used by all students, whatever their professional background
c. it should be easy to understand, even out of context
d. it should be interesting and (of course) possible to translate.

In short, I have tried to produce a book which will give an overview both of the main issues of translation and of the English language.

5 Principles of translation

Although this is not a theoretical work, I realize that teachers may appreciate some guidelines on how to help the students evaluate their own work. Specific remarks are given in the *Comments* after each activity. Below are some general principles which are relevant to all translation:

a. *Meaning*. The translation should reflect accurately the meaning of the original text. Nothing should be arbitrarily added or removed, though occasionally part of the meaning can be 'transposed', for example, He was *limp* with fatigue might become: Il était tellement fatigué qu'il *ne tenait plus debout*. Ask yourself:
   – is the meaning of the original text clear? if not, where does the uncertainty lie?
   – are any words 'loaded', that is, are there any underlying implications? ('Correct me if I'm wrong . . .' suggests 'I know I'm right'!)
   – is the dictionary meaning of a particular word the most suitable one? (should *subverzija* be *subversion* in English?)
   – does anything in the translation sound unnatural or forced?
b. *Form*. The ordering of words and ideas in the translation should match the original as closely as possible. (This is particularly important in translating legal documents, guarantees, contracts, etc.) But differences in language structure often require changes

in the form and order of words. When in doubt, underline in the original text the words on which the main stress falls. (See activities 1.3, 2.1, and 2.2.)

c. *Register.* Languages often differ greatly in their levels of formality in a given context (say, the business letter). To resolve these differences, the translator must distinguish between formal or fixed expressions (*Je vous prie, madame, d'agréer l'expression de mes sentiments distingués,* or *Please find enclosed* . . .) and personal expressions, in which the writer or speaker sets the tone.

Consider also:
 – would any expression in the original sound too formal/ informal, cold/warm, personal/impersonal . . . if translated literally?
 – what is the intention of the speaker or writer? (to persuade/ dissuade, apologize/criticize?) Does this come through in the translation?

d. *Source language influence.* One of the most frequent criticisms of translation is that 'it doesn't sound natural'. This is because the translator's thoughts and choice of words are too strongly moulded by the original text. A good way of shaking off the source language (SL) influence is to set the text aside and translate a few sentences aloud, from memory. This will suggest natural patterns of thought in the first language (L1), which may not come to mind when the eye is fixed on the SL text.

e. *Style and clarity.* The translator should not change the style of the original. But if the text is sloppily written, or full of tedious repetitions, the translator may, for the reader's sake, correct the defects.

f. *Idiom.* Idiomatic expressions are notoriously untranslatable. These include similes, metaphors, proverbs and sayings (*as good as gold*), jargon, slang, and colloquialisms (*user-friendly, the Big Apple, yuppie,* etc.), and (in English) phrasal verbs. If the expressions cannot be directly translated, try any of the following:
 – retain the original word, in inverted commas: *'yuppie'*
 – retain the original expression, with a literal explanation in brackets: *Indian summer* (dry, hazy weather in late autumn)
 – use a close equivalent: *talk of the devil* = *vuk na vratima* (literally, 'the wolf at the door')
 – use a non-idiomatic or plain prose translation: *a bit over the top* = *un peu excessif.*

The golden rule is: if the idiom does not work in the L1, do not force it into the translation.

(The principles outlined above are adapted from Frederick Fuller: *The Translator's Handbook.* For more detailed comments, see Peter Newmark: *Approaches to Translation.*)

Last words

A few years ago, I was asked to give a short talk on translation to a
general audience at The British Council in Dhaka, Bangladesh. I
turned over various titles in my mind, but they all seemed wrong.
In the end, I opted for the obvious: 'Problems of Translation'.
After the talk (which was well attended in spite of the title!), a lady
from the audience came up to me and said, 'You know, I actually
enjoyed it!' Then she added quickly, 'I must tell you: just as I was
leaving home my young daughter asked me where I was going. I
told her "to hear somebody talking about translation." "Oh," she
said, "is that an interesting story?"'

I think it is.

How to use this book

> Translation, unfortunately, is something you learn only by doing.
>
> (William Weaver, translator of *The Name of the Rose*)

Translation is designed to be used by teachers and students from any language background who are involved in the study of English. The aim of the book is to provide the teacher with a wide range of translation activities devised specifically for language learners.

The main concern of the book is not how to teach translation, but how to use translation in teaching, as one approach among many in the language class.

All the material is in English, and is drawn from many different subject areas. However, no specialist knowledge of any subject is required. Nor need you or your students have any previous experience of translating.

The book is addressed to you, the teacher, but the material in the activities is presented ready for use with the students.

Translation is primarily intended for work with students whose mother tongue is not English, but who have a sound grasp of the language (Intermediate level and above). The book may also be used with students of other languages who have sufficient competence in English, and with professionals (scientists, doctors, lawyers, journalists, etc.) whose work involves the use of English.

As a resource book for the teacher, *Translation* offers not only material ready-made for use in class, but also guidelines on the language focus of each activity. And, most important, it introduces the teacher to general strategies which can be adapted to other materials in order to keep the class work fresh and varied.

The role of the teacher

Some of the teachers who use this book will, I am aware, be experienced translators themselves. Others may have done only the occasional translation. And, again, some may regularly use translation in their teaching, while others may never have tried it – but would like to.

I have therefore designed the book in such a way that it can easily be used by both kinds of teacher. Those with less experience will be able to use the material as it is, ready-prepared. While teachers who have already developed techniques of their own will, I hope, find in *Translation* many useful new approaches to supplement their work. This, after all, is one of the main functions of a resource book.

Below are some brief comments on the teacher's role in using *Translation*.

1 Finding and presenting material

The sets of texts and passages in the book have been carefully laid out in task sheets as examples or, in some cases, so that they can be photocopied for direct use with the students. (Please respect the notes on copyright restrictions.) You should not feel obliged to use all the texts. And, of course, you are most welcome to add material of your own. In the *Comments* to certain activities, I have indicated where suitable material can be found.

For many of the activities, particularly in section 5, the students can be asked to contribute material from other sources.

2 In class

An essential feature of all the activities is group discussion. At first, the students may call on you to intervene (or interfere!) at too early a stage. Explain to them that it is more profitable if you reserve your own opinion until later in the discussion.

Your role, however, will not be that of a passive spectator. Try circulating from group to group. Some of the weaker students may need help in understanding the English. This is best given indirectly, not by translating for the students but by listening to their translations and pointing out any features of the English that have not come through. With the better students, listen carefully, taking notes. Then, in the second stage of the discussion (when one group meets another), bring together groups which have found different solutions.

In the final stage – class discussion – your contribution is vital. After listening to the suggested translations, indicate your preferences (there may be several), give your reasons, and, if you wish, offer your own alternative translations. Here, it is worth recalling Henry Gifford's words: 'The first law of translation is clear: nothing can be taken as final.'

3 Pair/group work

As I mentioned earlier, translation is usually regarded as an activity to be done on one's own. Why then translate with other people?

The answer is that translation is naturally suited to discussion. The questions the translator usually solves alone are questions worth discussing with others. For language practice, translation need not be done in isolation.

Most of the activities are based on work-in pairs or small groups. The purpose of this is to give the students a chance to be heard, to test their ideas against those of others, and to listen and compare. One of the teacher's main tasks in the group work is to control the language of discussion. Since the students will naturally want to use the mother tongue in discussion, try to ensure that they do not forget the starting-point, which is the text in English. All discussion should refer back to the text.

4 Language correction

One of my aims in this book has been to relieve the teacher of the burden of correcting too much written translation. In these activities, much of the correction is done by the students themselves, and on oral translation. There are two advantages to this:

a. because the students are pooling their suggestions, and listening to each other, they are more receptive to any corrections given (they are learning from each other's mistakes)

b. the teacher is no longer caught in the trap of having to correct the same errors twenty or thirty times over (as happens with written translation); here, one comment is good for all.

I am not suggesting, however, that we dispense altogether with written translation. It must be done, and needs to be corrected. My one word of advice would be this: correction means marking not only the errors but also the *trouvailles* – the intelligent solutions. Translation takes time and effort. The occasional tick ($\checkmark$) relieves the monotony of underlining in red, and gives the student much-needed encouragement.

5 The use of dictionaries

There is no need to ban the dictionary from the class. However, I feel that for the activities in this book it is not needed. The dictionary tends to make the students less resourceful, because they take the entry as the final word, and do not explore other possibilities.

6 Some problems

Fatigue. Translation is demanding, and often frustrating. Do not be surprised if at times the students go for the easy solution, or quite simply give up. If a group becomes blocked, suggest that they move on to fresh material, or else put them together with a group that has found a solution.

Translation is a process of thought and *afterthought*. The best ideas may occur later.

Disagreement. There will be disagreement, at times quite violent. As the teacher, you will probably be expected to arbitrate. Most disputes can be settled by reason – and particularly by referring back to the original text. However, if agreement cannot be reached, try listing the contentious sentences on a wall-chart, and leave them there for the students to add their own suggestions over the weeks.

Discipline. This means not class discipline, but mental discipline. In the discussion groups, it will inevitably happen that some students will be content to paraphrase, rather than translate. If this occurs, you may need to insist on full written translations, rather than the working notes I have suggested.

Working speeds. In any group, there will be both hares and tortoises, sprinters and plodders. Some students will be frustrated if they are kept waiting, others if they are broken off before they have finished. This frustration can be avoided either by allowing the groups to join up for discussion in their own time, when they are ready, or by setting strict time limits and asking the students to do as much as they can in the time.

How the book is organized

The book is divided into five sections of roughly equal length. Each section concentrates on a particular area of language which closely concerns the translator. The five main areas are:

1 **Context and register**
2 **Word order and reference**
3 **Time: tense, mood, and aspect**
4 **Concepts and notions**
5 **Idiom: from one culture to another**

These divisions enable you to find an activity suited to a specific purpose. If the students need practice in, for instance, the use of the article in English, or of referential words such as *it, that, which,* suitable material can be found in activities 2.4 or 2.6.

The basic structure of the sections is more or less identical. Each consists of between four and nine independent activities, all related to aspects of the general theme.

How each activity is organized

The activities are presented under three main headings:
Preparation, In class, and *Comments.*

Preparation
Under *Preparation*, you will find a brief indication of the kind of material required (and provided), and instructions for any changes to be made to the text (for instance, words to be omitted).

In class
In class work covers warm-up activities directly related to the translation work that follows, and translation and discussion of the texts provided.

Comments
The *Comments* are provided to help you and your students to understand the purpose of the activity, and to point out some of the problems that might arise.

Variations
Some activities have variations that can be used with different materials or longer texts.

Material
Each activity contains sufficient material in the form of task sheets for 30–45 minutes' work (and often more). My aim has been to provide you with a firm starting-point, that is, sufficient material to try out the activity. Later, changes and additions can (and should) be made.

The material is of two kinds:

a. shorter texts (on average, three to four sentences), chosen primarily for in-class translation and discussion work
b. longer texts, to be translated out of class but later discussed in class.

Context
In translating, it is essential to know from what context a particular passage has been drawn (an academic article, a book of memoirs, a news broadcast, a political speech, or a satire).

Clearly, it is not possible to give the students the full context of each extract. To avoid unnecessary confusion I have:

– provided the source/title for every extract, however short
– italicized those expressions in the text on which the students need to concentrate
– made no alterations to the original wording; any cuts, for the sake of brevity, are indicated by three dots (. . .)
– given as much of the surrounding context as seemed necessary for accurate translation.

Language level
In *Translation* we are dealing with two language levels:

a. The complexity or 'difficulty' of English as the source language.
b. The level of competence required to convert the English into another language.

These are complex questions which cannot be resolved simply by consulting convenient word lists. The word *anosmia*, for instance, would be unlikely to appear in a graded textbook for Intermediate students. Yet it is not 'difficult' to translate, as in:

> Thousands of people lose the sense of smell every year. This phenomenon is known medically as 'anosmia'.

While a beginner's -level word, such as *say* could not be translated without some thought in a context such as:

> 'Mrs Moore, what is this echo?'
> 'Don't you know?'
> 'No – what is it? Oh, *do say*!'

In short: the difficulties of the translator are not always the same as those of the language learner.

In general, the English corresponds to Cambridge Proficiency level. However, in almost all the sets of material I have included passages which could easily be used with First Certificate or Intermediate students. But what is 'easy' and what is 'difficult' must be decided through translation.

1 Context and register

Introduction

Why, you may wonder, does this book begin with *context* and *register*, and not with something more straightforward and clear-cut, like *the present simple* or *prefixes* and *suffixes*? And, anyway, what is context? What is register? And what bearing do they have on translation?

Instead of offering plausible-sounding definitions (which would probably make the matter no clearer), I shall try to answer these questions by means of examples, and from the examples draw some brief conclusions.

But let me first make one, possibly obvious, general point: all language must occur somewhere, and all language is intended to be read or heard by someone. Even an internal monologue is addressed to someone – the speaker. Since all words are shaped by their context, we can say – very broadly – that context comes before language. This is why context has been chosen as our starting point.

Does context really matter?

Or, to put the question differently, is not 'knowing the rules' what matters most?

Let us think for a moment of an exercise still often used in teaching the mother tongue – the so-called 'composition'. Pupils are set a topic with a title such as 'Rain', 'A summer's day', 'My most exciting experience'. The result is usually something like this:

> I like the rain in summer, especially when thunderstorms suddenly break over the nearby hills. And in autumn, when it falls softly on the orchard and brings out the scent of the fallen leaves. But most of all, I like the first spring rain that chases away the winter . . .

And so on. A dull, dutiful piece of writing, which will get 'good marks' because it has few mistakes. But it is a language of no place. It has no context and therefore no character. This is not the child's fault, because the task is an almost impossible one: to write without a reason (other than producing a piece of writing) and without a real reader in mind (the teacher is not a 'real' reader). The flaw lies in the task itself: the titles given do not suggest a *context*. As Hedge (1988) says in her introduction to *Writing* (OUP Resource Books for Teachers), 'Most of the writing we do in real life is written with a reader in mind . . . Knowing who the reader is provides the writer with a context without which it is difficult to know exactly what or how to write'.

Context matters, then, because if we have no context in mind we cannot give proper shape to our thoughts. Very simply, we do not know which words to choose because we do not know who they are intended for. The context helps to determine our choice. Which is why if I were, for instance, paying a subscription I might send a note with the words: '*Enclosed please find* a cheque for £50', but I would not send my son or daughter a note saying: '*Enclosed please find* £5 for your pocket money.'

To summarize: what I mean by context is the *what, where,* and *to whom* of our communication – *what* we are writing or speaking about (subject matter), *where* the language occurs (place or publication), and *to whom* it is addressed. All three are relevant in translation.

Unwritten rules

One of the particular concerns of this section is with what I would call the 'unwritten rules' of language. That is, not the rules of grammar but the patterns – and constraints – of usage. In almost all languages there are words and expressions which are regularly, even automatically, associated with specific contexts. For instance: *Press down to release* (instructions), *In the author's opinion* . . . (academic article), *scattered thundershowers* (weather report), *Ci-inclus, veuillez trouver* . . . (business letter), *an outstanding example of* . . . (brochure/guide-book), *light refreshments will be served* (notice/circular letter).

There are no rules which prevent us from using expressions such as these in other contexts. Yet why is it that two villagers talking about the weather would be unlikely to speak of 'scattered thundershowers'? And why would a hostess, at an informal party, be unlikely to tell her friends that 'light refreshments will now be served'?

The simplest answer is, surely, that we are following the rules of usage. And these are largely unwritten. There is no rule that says we cannot speak of 'scattered thundershowers' in a love-letter or in an academic thesis, though it might sound odd if we did.

What happens if we try to break these unwritten rules? And do they really exist? Let us take a test case. Would you expect to find the following sentence in a tourist brochure, a scientific article, or neither?

> Samples of sand taken from the sun-kissed, palm-fringed beaches of Goa revealed abnormally high concentrations of sodium chloride.

The most likely answer is neither. This, of course, is a made-up sentence, yet it is not an impossible one. But there is no rule which prevents a scientist from speaking of *sunkissed beaches*, or which says that tourist brochures cannot mention the concentrations of sodium chloride. We can only say that the language is unusual in either context.

If it is important in the mother tongue to be aware of these unwritten rules, it is doubly important when dealing with translation. For in translation we are following not one but two sets of unwritten rules, and they do not always overlap. To take just one example: a circular letter addressed to residents of a housing complex might contain (in English) expressions such as: '*Kindly use* the plastic bags provided for rubbish disposal' or '*It would be appreciated if* residents would not park in the entrance road.' In another language, it might be natural to use 'blunter' language in a similar context, for example: '*You must use* . . .' and '*Parking is forbidden* . . .'.

The context is the same, but not the register.

Register

If context is the *what, where,* and *to whom,* then register is the *how.* How do we express ourselves in a given context? If the scientist quoted in activity 1.4 uses an expression such as: 'The sun *simply has no business* to be rotating as slowly as it does', he is signalling clearly through his language that the reader he has in mind is a non-scientist. And so, to reassure the reader, he drops into a colloquial style, although a more formal tone would be expected.

Once again, we are dealing with the unwritten rules. If we are struck by an expression such as *the sun simply has no business,* it is because it does not match the language we expect in the context of astrophysics. It is not 'formal enough', the register is 'too low'.

Register gives colour to language. To ignore it in translation is to translate the words rather than the meaning.

The activities

Since specific comments are given after each activity, I shall outline here only a few of the general questions raised in this section.

1 What is the relationship between context and language? Why do we associate certain expressions (*narrow winding streets, from the foregoing . . ., the intentness of her gaze, press upward with thumbs*) with certain contexts?

2 What clues or signals do we pick up from language, even without knowing the context? Can we identify the clues? Would they be the

same in our own language? (See activity 1.1.)

3 Is the language of the passage consistent? If not, what is 'out of place', and why? Would the tone (register) be the same in the first language (L1)? (See activities 1.4 and 1.5.)

4 How clear is the meaning? Is anything meant but not said? (See activity 1.3.)

5 How literally should the words be taken? Should the translation be literal or idiomatic?

1.1 Context clues

PREPARATION

1 From a variety of sources, make a selection of very short passages in which some feature of the language gives a clue to the context (*enclosed please find* (formal letter), *with the gradual expansion of trade there emerged* (history book), etc.).

2 Extract from each passage a fragment of text, as in the examples above. Write up the fragments on the blackboard or on an overhead transparency (OHT).

3 A variation that can be used as a warm-up to this task is to give the students similar fragments from the mother tongue to work with.

IN CLASS

1 Ask the students to work in groups of three. They should suggest a possible source for each fragment (tourist brochure, news report, medical article), and note down any words that give a clue to the context.

2 Each group should then discuss its suggestions with another.

3 As a round-up, run through the fragments with the whole class, noting their suggestions next to each. Before revealing the sources, allow some time for discussion of any strong points of disagreement.

4 Then give the students the source and full text of each fragment.

COMMENTS

1 The point of this activity is to discuss what words can suggest to us – even out of context. Why do we associate certain expressions with one context rather than another? What 'clues' are we picking up? It is important, then, to place the emphasis on searching for clues rather than discovering the right answer.

2 When we translate we already know, of course, what the context is – what kind of work we are dealing with and who it is intended for, and we translate accordingly. But it is still useful to look more closely at what we are taking for granted, that is, at the language we normally associate with a particular context. For, if we are not aware of the language we expect, we are less able to react to the unexpected.

TASK SHEET

Below are some fragments of language taken from different contexts. Suggest a possible source for each (a TV weather report, notes on a record sleeve, a book review). Compare your suggestions with those of others in the group, and then with the actual sources.

1 . . . a cool, dry place. Keep well out of . . .
2 . . . acknowledge the assistance of my colleagues, and lastly . . .
3 . . . magnificent vistas of coastline, beautiful beaches, . . .
4 . . . my whole body is caressed by a protective, creamy moisturizer . . .
5 . . . an octagon with a central pillar and spacious windows . . .
6 . . . smooth, slick, and atmospheric, . . .
7 . . . the Canadians were hammered . . .
8 . . . gazed out over her dark garden. The soft Normandy breeze, . . .
9 . . . bringing scattered thundershowers . . .
10 . . . opens with a sad little melody . . .
11 A sizzling saga set in . . .
12 . . . faces stern new tests in coming months.
13 Simmer gently . .
14 . . . by depressing one of the buttons . . .
15 Arrived Leopoldville. Met at terminus by M, . . .
16 Trap for catching birds or animals, esp. one made . . .
17 Carriage hereunder is subject to . . .

SOURCES

1 Store in . . . Keep well out of reach of children.
(standard instruction on medicine boxes)

2 I should also like to . . . of my wife, whose tact and common sense have been invaluable throughout.
(Bertrand Russell: *The Problems of Philosophy*)

3 Situated at the crossroads of western, central, and eastern Europe, Yugoslavia offers . . . the clear waters of the Adriatic, as well as unspoilt pine forests and tranquil lakes.
(PanAdriatic Travel tourist brochure)

4 When I bathe in Fenjal, . . . leaving my skin silky soft and sensuously smooth.
(advertisement for Fenjal bath oil)

5 Salisbury chapter-house of about 1275 is centrally planned, . . . filling the walls entirely except for the arcade strip.
(Nikolaus Pevsner: *An Outline of European Architecture*)

6 The three-part adaptation of Mr Gavin Lyall's story was . . . though as usual it rather overdid the Oxford scenes.
(television review, *The Listener*)

7 Meanwhile, . . . 15–6, 15–3, 15–9 by Cuba in the final.
(sports report on volleyball, *The Guardian*)

8 She padded on bare feet to the open window and . . . laden with fragrance, fondled her long black hair.
(*In Love and Friendship*, quoted in SHE *magazine*)

9 During the afternoon, the wind will strengthen from the west, . . . to coastal parts of Devon and Cornwall.
(BBC weather report)

10 The first movement . . . which asserts the key of C minor and is followed by a dialogue between the upper and lower woodwind.
(notes on a record sleeve)

11 . . . in the wanton world of the outrageously rich.
(back-cover blurb for a thriller)

12 The Congress Party, which took an electoral hammering in 1987, . . .
(article on Indian politics, *The Guardian*)

13 . . . until the peel is nearly soft.
(Marguerite Patten: *500 Recipes – Jams, Pickles, Chutneys*)

14 Select the waveband . . . and tune in the required station.
(operating instructions for Grundig radio-cassette)

15 . . . who took me to hotel.
(Graham Greene: *Congo Journal* – diary of an African journey)

16 snare *n.*, & *v.t.* 1. *n.* . . . with noose of wire or cord.
(*The Concise Oxford Dictionary*)

17 . . . the rules and limitations relating to liability established by the Warsaw Convention.
(IATA – conditions of travel on airline ticket)

"Tomorrow will be in the low seventies with scattered showers"

1.2 Matching pairs

PREPARATION

1 Collect material similar to that described in activity 1.1, consisting of sentences or very short passages suitable for division into two parts. Each half should contain some feature which would give a clue to the source:

> Like all varieties *in our range*, it's *packed with mouthwatering* ingredients. (advertisement)

2 Prepare and present the material in the form of two task sheets. Task sheet A should contain the first half, task sheet B the second half of each passage. (The two halves are not given in matching order.) Make enough copies of the task sheets for half of the class.

3 As a warm-up to this task you may like to give the students similar matching pairs in their own language.

IN CLASS

1 Divide the class into two large groups, A and B. In each group, the students form into pairs.

2 Give the pairs in group A task sheet A material, those in group B, task sheet B.

3 Ask the students to discuss in pairs the probable source of each of their fragments. The sources should be noted as precisely as possible: not just 'a speech', but 'an after-dinner speech', not just 'a book' but 'a novel, possibly translated from the Russian', etc.

4 When the students are ready, ask each pair to join with a pair from the other group (A goes to B, or B to A). They must not show each other their passages.

5 First, they compare their lists of possible sources, noting any differences or doubts. Then, taking their passages in turn, each pair describes to the other what kind of 'missing half' it is looking for. (Those with set A are looking for the completion of a sentence, those with set B for the opening.) Only after this rough description has been given should the matching half be shown.

COMMENTS

1 Here, as in the previous activity, one of the aims is to make students more conscious of the link between language and context. Why is it that expressions such as *scattered thundershowers, simmer gently, mouthwatering ingredients, depress the button, laden with fragrance, subject to the rules* are all so strongly associated with a particular kind of writing or speech and with a particular context?

Language conforms to two sets of rules, those of grammar, and those of customary usage. Students are generally well trained in the former, but left to fend for themselves with the latter. This activity should help to bring out more clearly the 'unwritten rules' of language.

2 If you have not already done the warm-up, one possible follow-up to this is to give the students similar matching halves in their own language.

TASK SHEET A   Discuss with your partner the probable source of the fragments
below.

1 Central banks intervene massively . . .
2 The rich heritage of the city has given birth to . . .
3 When I was honoured by the invitation . . .
4 A fine, distinguished country residence.
5 Towards the end of November, during a thaw, at nine o'clock
 one morning . . .
6 Like all varieties in our range, it's . . .
7 There are entertaining character sketches of the learned world,
 and also of members of his family, and . . .
8 Tuesday night. At one a.m. we were ready.
9 I will finish by repeating our very sincere thanks to Hugh
 Dickinson for . . .
10 Further research may show that the range of diseases responsive
 to the treatment include . . .
11 If war, threat of war, civil unrest, industrial action, or any other
 event outside the control of the Company either delays or
 extends the holiday . . .
12 A substantial employer in Central London has vacancies for
 linguists who wish to make daily practical use of their
 languages. They will be . . .
13 The two pillars of his performing art rest on . . .

TASK SHEET B   Discuss with your partner the probable source of the fragments
below.

1 . . . based in Central London and will be expected to maintain
 fluency in reading, writing, and understanding their chosen
 language. Candidates should be over 21, with a thorough
 knowledge of Bulgarian or Czech.
2 . . . the marvellous way in which he proposed the toast of the
 College and entertained us and enlightened us in so doing.
 Thank you very much indeed.
3 We had taken off our handcuffs and opened up the hole.
 Ssekalo climbed on to the boxes and Okech lifted him up and
 pushed him into the ventilator.
4 . . . we cannot accept liability for any resulting loss, damage or
 expense and any refund will be subject to the deduction of
 reasonable expenses.

5 . . . a perfect understanding of the styles of differing periods and an exceptionally plastic conducting technique.

6 . . . heart disease, obesity, schizophrenia, rheumatoid arthritis, and multiple sclerosis.

7 . . . to prop up falling dollar.

8 . . . the whole is suffused by his belief in the potential of medical research.

9 . . . packed with mouthwatering ingredients.

10 . . . a train on the Warsaw and Petersburg railway was approaching the latter city at full speed.

11 . . . to give this year's Ernest Jones lecture, I felt, of course, the usual mixture of trepidation and pride.

12 Offers over £300,000.

13 . . . superb handicrafts executed by craftsmen whose ancestors wrought miracles in marble.

SOURCES

The consecutive numbers below refer to task sheet A; the number of the matching passage from task sheet B is given in brackets.

1 Headline, *The Guardian* (B7)

2 American Express, *A Guide to Agra* (B13)

3 E. H. Gombrich, opening words of a public lecture on art history (B11)

4 Estate agent's advertisement for a house (B12)

5 Opening sentence of a chapter in Dostoievsky's novel *The Brothers Karamazov*, English translation (B10)

6 Advertisement for *Heinz 57 Varieties* (B9)

7 Review in *The Guardian* of the autobiography of Peter Medawar, Nobel prize-winner for science (B8)

8 *An Escape from Kampala*, autobiographical account of an escape from prison, Wycliffe Kato in *Granta 22* (B3)

9 Dinner speech by Sir Andrew Huxley, Master of Trinity College, Cambridge, in Trinity College *Annual Record* (B2)

10 Science report, *The Times* (B6)

11 Extract from 'Booking conditions' in a brochure from PanAdriatic Travel (B4)

12 Advertisement for the post of Linguist/Translator, in *The Linguist* (B1)

13 Sleeve-notes to a Hungarian (Qualiton) recording of Mozart's symphonies, conducted by János Ferencsik (B5)

1.3 Implications

1 Choose short passages in which certain expressions are marked off (by the writer) in inverted commas, for one or other of the reasons set out in step 1 below (not simply as quotations of what someone has already said). For instance:

> People seem to feel that there is some essential difference between beggars and ordinary '*working*' men.

2 Prepare enough task sheets A and B for half the class.

1 Ask the students to work in pairs, with one set of examples each. Before translating, they should discuss why they think the expressions have been marked off. To help focus the discussion, write up a few prompt-questions:

Is the expression placed in inverted commas because it is:
– *unexpected in the context?*
– *meant to be read with a (vocal) stress?*
– *deliberately used in two senses?*
– *used ironically, playfully, disparagingly . . . ?*

2 The students note down their translations for the sentences in which words in inverted commas appear. (The surrounding context can be translated orally.)

3 Each pair compares notes with others who have worked on the same set.

4 (Optional) Each pair joins with another which has worked on a different set. In turn, they offer oral translations for each other's examples, and then compare and discuss the differences.

1 This task requires close reading of the immediate context. Many of the expressions marked off by the writer refer either backwards or forwards to other parts of the text. A good example is the first sentence in task sheet B.

> We talk of 'falling in love', but the process is usually *slower than this would suggest*.

To make sense of the words in italics, the translator needs to find an expression which will suggest – as the English does – that falling in love happens quickly! Likewise, in task sheet A, number 4, the translator will have to make sure that the expression 'free patients' is logically linked to the words *They didn't pay*:

> . . . it was usual for 'free patients' to have their teeth extracted with no anaesthetic. They didn't pay, so why should they have an anaesthetic . . .

2 Remind the students that they do not always have to follow the English use of inverted commas. Other devices might be more natural in their own language (altering the word order, repeating words, etc.), in which case, they should be used.

3 See also section 2, activity 2.1.

TASK SHEET A

In each of the passages below, certain words are marked off by inverted commas, for instance 'Cape Wrath doesn't mean "angry",' Mr Mathers said. Why do you think attention is drawn to these words? Is it because they have more than one meaning? Or because they are unusual in the context? Or perhaps because special emphasis is intended?

With a partner, discuss the examples in your set, and suggest translations for each expression in inverted commas. Also decide whether the inverted commas are needed in the translation.

1 'Cape Wrath doesn't mean "angry",' Mr Mathers said. 'It's from a Norse word that means "turning-point". This is where the ships turned south.'
(Paul Theroux: *The Kingdom by the Sea*)

2 When do you open your Christmas presents?
Open them only in the privacy of your own family. Do remember to leave the receipts in 'by mistake', then everyone can change everything next week.
(*SHE* magazine)

3 A good actor cannot merely imagine a given situation but can 'feel' what it would be like in such a situation. Art without feeling is dead.
(C. J. Adcock: *Fundamentals of Psychology*)

4 Well into this century it was usual for 'free' patients at the big hospitals to have their teeth extracted with no anaesthetic. They didn't pay, so why should they have an anaesthetic – that was the attitude.
(George Orwell: *Collected Essays*)

5 (From a report on the opening of a new Civic Hall) When the word 'civic' was revived in the nineteenth century it got off to a bad start. Intended to inspire memories of the Roman Republic, it in fact came to mean 'pompous', 'small-minded' and 'parochial'. A building of this sort (the new Civic Hall) should help to set the word off on a new and more hopeful tack.
(*Architectural Review*)

6 In West Germany, researchers have implanted artificial bone, made from the tiny skeletons of algae, into the jaws of laboratory animals. They say that algal 'bone' behaves better than the synthetic material surgeons currently use to mend damage to bone tissue in humans.
(*New Scientist*)

TASK SHEET B

In each of the passages below, certain words are marked off by inverted commas, for instance, 'falling in love'. Why do you think attention is drawn to these words? Is it because they have more than one meaning? Or because they are unusual in the context? Or perhaps because special emphasis is intended?

With a partner, discuss the examples in your set, and suggest translations for each expression in inverted commas. Also decide whether the inverted commas are needed in the translation.

1 We talk of 'falling in love', but the process is usually slower than this would suggest. Usually it takes time to build up a firm sentiment, but various factors may speed up the process.
(C. J. Adcock: *Fundamentals of Psychology*)

2 One of the words which to an Englishman conjures up the quintessence of embarrassment is a 'scene'. But in the Middle East and elsewhere in the South, 'scenes' between people explode continually in public and in private. They die down again just as quickly, leaving behind no 'atmosphere'.
(Anthony Parsons in *The Listener*)

3 I remember the slightly self-conscious Sunday afternoon, when I was nineteen, and I 'composed' my first two 'poems'.
(D. H. Lawrence: *Phoenix*)

4 When the experimental psychologist talks of 'emotive behaviour', he nearly always refers to rage, fear, sex, and hunger, whereas emotions which do not beget overt activity are slurred over as 'moods' or sentiments – with the implication that they are a suspect category of pseudo-emotions unworthy of the scientist's attention.
(Arthur Koestler: *The Act of Creation*)

1.4 Alternatives

PREPARATION

1 You will need to find a number of short passages (ten to fifteen lines), preferably ones which contain a mixture of formal and informal language, or which combine technical and colloquial expressions, such as:

> Physicists are well used to *surprises being thrown up* by quantum theory.

If the context from which the passage is drawn is not immediately clear, it should be given (brochure, public lecture, radio talk, etc.).

2 Prepare enough copies so that each student has one.

IN CLASS

1 Ask the students to work in groups of three on any one of the passages you have chosen, or those in task sheets A, B, and C. They

should read through the passage together, consider the alternatives, and then (individually) mark them in order of preference; for example, if they write: *1 a), c), b)*, it means alternative *a)* was most preferred, *b)* least.

2 The students then discuss the reasons for their choices.

3 Next, the groups exchange texts, and work on the new material as before.

4 When the students have finished, give them the original wording.

COMMENTS

1 Translation is not actually required in this activity, though in the discussion the students may want to try out some of the alternatives in their own language to see how they would work. This they should feel free to do.

2 This activity is deliberately called *Alternatives* to indicate that each of the choices offered is possible. The aim is not to guess correctly which expression the writer used, but to think through different ways of conveying the same ideas. In this sense, the activity differs considerably from a multiple-choice exercise, in which only one of the answers is the right one. An alternative is neither right nor wrong, merely different.

3 Particularly suitable for this activity is material which naturally combines spoken and written idioms (letters and circulars, radio talks, public lectures, etc., as in the *Variation*). Many of the texts in section 4 are drawn from such sources and could be adapted to this activity. (See also activity 5.1.)

TASK SHEET A

Read through the paragraph below and consider the three alternatives, a), b), and c). Rank them in order of preference and discuss the reasons for your choice with the others in your group.

The (1). . . slow rotation speed of the sun gives a revealing and subtle clue to the mystery of the origin of the planets. The sun (2) . . . to be rotating as slowly as it actually does. Instead of spinning round once in about 26 days, as in fact it does, our expectation would be that it should rotate in as little as a few hours. You might be tempted to think that the calculations must be (3) . . . . But we can see that (4) . . ., because many stars do in fact rotate around in a few hours, just as the calculations show they should.
(Fred Hoyle: *The Nature of the Universe*)

1 a) amazingly   b) exceptionally   c) extremely

2 a) simply has no business   b) ought not, in principle   c) would
not be expected

3 a) inaccurate   b) wildly wrong   c) erroneous

4 a) this is not the case   b) things are not too bad   c) the figures
are not wholly incorrect

TASK SHEET B

Read through the paragraph below and consider the three
alternatives, a), b), and c). Rank them in order of preference and
discuss the reasons for your choice with the others in your group.

Another ancient survival is the strange business of 'backs to the
wall' when feeding in public. Observe diners arriving at any
restaurant and you will see them (1) . . . the wall seats. No one ever
(2) . . . a centre table in an open space. Open seating positions are
only taken when all the wall seats are already occupied. This dates
back to (3) . . . of avoiding sudden attack during the deep
concentration (4) . . . .

(Desmond Morris: *Manwatching*)

1 a) head for   b) make a bee-line for   c) direct themselves
towards

2 a) goes straight to   b) voluntarily selects   c) deliberately
chooses

3 a) a primeval feeding practice   b) an old survival tactic   c) the
primitive habit

4 a) needed for eating   b) involved in consuming food   c) that
goes with feeding

TASK SHEET C

Read through the paragraph below and consider the three
alternatives a), b), c), and d). Rank them in order of preference and
discuss the reasons for your choice with the others in your group.

Electroshock therapy was (1) . . . in Glasgow when I was a medical
student. Its introduction was (2) . . . opposed by some of the senior
psychiatrists, including my first teacher, Dr Sclare. He illustrated
his objections by (3) . . . a woman of twenty-six who had begun a
career as a concert violinist. At the end of her first, very successful
tour she had (4) . . . depression, and it was felt that it would be a
pity if she didn't (5) . . . fairly soon. So she (6) . . . a course of
electric shocks which brightened her up. But unfortunately (one of

the common side-effects of these things), she forgot her violin repertoire. In those days (1949), in Glasgow, most of the senior psychiatrists (7) . . . electric shocks.

(R. D. Laing: *The Facts of Life*)

1 a) in its experimental phase   b) being tried out   c) on the way in

2 a) bitterly   b) resolutely   c) consistently

3 a) telling me about   b) citing the case of   c) alluding to

4 a) succumbed to nervous   b) crashed into a   c) manifested symptoms of

5 a) recover   b) recuperate   c) get going again   d)   show signs of improvement

6 a) underwent   b) got   c) was submitted to   d) followed

7 a) openly disapproved of   b) in principle rejected
   c) wouldn't have anything to do with

KEY TO TASKS

The original expressions used by the writers are:

Task sheet A 1a   2a   3b   4b
Task sheet B 1b   2b   3a   4b
Task sheet C 1b   2a   3a   4b   5c   6b   7c

VARIATION

Use similar material, but choose longer texts.

PREPARATION

1 Prepare at least one text for each student.

2 Ask the students to work on the text(s) out of class. After selecting the alternative they prefer in each case, they should translate the passage(s) in writing (using the alternatives chosen).

IN CLASS

1 Working in groups of four, the students compare translations, noting strong points of difference or similarity.

2 When they have finished, give them the original wording.

COMMENTS

1 It is important to suggest that all the alternatives are plausible, that is, they are expressions the writer might have used. The purpose of the activity is, so to speak, to 'get into the writer's skin' – to think with the writer. This is the first step in all translation.

2 This variation is a useful preparation for work on *Reformulations* and *Choice of Words* (see section 5).

3 This activity can also be used for translation into English. Find material in the mother tongue which has been redrafted or reworded (letters, circulars, programmes, conference brochures, etc.). Present the text to the students with alternatives for certain reworded passages. After choosing the alternative they prefer, they translate the text into English.

BBC
BRISTOL Network Production Centre

TO THE RESIDENTS OF WINDSOR TERRACE AND WINDSOR PLACE

Dear (1) _____

I am writing to give you advance information that we will be in your area recording a sequence for the new series of 'Casualty' (2) _____ on BBC 1 this Autumn.

The scenes are set in no.3 Windsor Terrace. The recording will take place on Thursday 27th August from 0830 until 1830 hours. Our recording unit will arrive at 0700 hours and we (3) _____ by 1930 hours. In the process we hope to cause as little disruption as possible, but, (4) _____ ,there will inevitably be (5) _____ for the brief time we are with you, for which we apologise in advance.

I hope that I shall have had the opportunity to meet you (6) _____ to explain that in order to keep the disturbance to a minimum we would be most grateful if car owners would (7) _____ in Windsor Place on Wednesday night. This is where we would need to park our large vehicles and we (8) _____ block in the cars of those hoping to leave for work! This will help speed up the operation enormously.

The series is based on the night shift of a Casualty unit and, naturally, all our recordings are done (9) _____ the Police and City Council.

We look forward to a successful recording, and if you have any queries, (10) _____ contact me on Bristol 556188.

(11) _____

Tony Rowe
Location Manager
Casualty

BBC BROADCASTING HOUSE   WHITELADIES ROAD   BRISTOL BS8 2LR
BRISTOL (0272) 732211   TELEX 265781 BSA   FACSIMILE (0272) 744114

TASK SHEET A   Read through the letter opposite and then translate it in writing, using the alternative, a), b), c), or d) you think best fits the context.

1 a) Sir/Madam   b) Resident   c) Neighbour

2 a) which you can see   b) due to be seen   c) to be shown   d) scheduled for presentation

3 a) hope to be through   b) expect to leave   c) should be finished

4 a) we must advise you   b) I'm afraid   c) as you can imagine

5 a) a degree of inconvenience   b) some disturbance   c) a fair amount of activity

6 a) in advance   b) before you read this   c) prior to the recording date

7 a) please refrain from parking   b) kindly not park   c) assist by not parking

8 a) don't want to   b) would not like to   c) do not wish to   d) would hate to

9 a) in full consultation with   b) with the kind assistance of   c) with the official approval of

10 a) I suggest you   b) please do not hesitate to   c) kindly   d) feel free to

11 a) Yours faithfully   b) Yours sincerely   c) Yours truly

TASK SHEET B   Read through the passage below. Then translate it in writing, using the alternative, a), b), c), or d), you think best fits the context.

Physicists are (1) . . . surprises (2) . . . quantum theory, as they try to understand the behaviour of the atomic world. Now two theoreticians, Dr John Donoghue and Dr Barry Holstein, of the University of Massachusetts, have found that the theory contradicts, (3) . . . in a very small way, one of the foundations of Einstein's theory of gravity – general relativity.

Paradoxically, however, it (4) . . .: that heavier objects fall to the ground quicker than light ones. Galileo is (5) . . . to have first shown experimentally that heavy and light objects reach the ground at the same time, by dropping objects off the Leaning Tower of Pisa.

The explanation of this is that heavy objects (6) . . . than light ones: they are more reluctant to (7) . . . the action of a force. So although they feel the force of gravity more strongly than light objects when flung off the tower, they are more reluctant to respond to it, and the two properties (8) . . .

Einstein made this apparent equality between 'inertial' mass and 'gravitational' mass of an object a (9) . . . of his theory of gravity. However, Drs Donoghue and Holstein have shown that, according to quantum theory, the inertial mass of heavier bodies is slightly lower than normally believed, (10) . . . to respond more readily to gravity and hence fall to the ground faster than light bodies.

The reason (11) . . ., again according to quantum theory, every charged particle, such as an electron, is surrounded by a cloud of massless particles called photons, the carriers of the electromagnetic field. This cloud changes the total energy, and (12) . . . mass, of the particle by an amount that depends on temperature.

(science report, *The Times*)

1 a) accustomed to   b) well used to   c) habituated to

2 a) thrown up by   b) generated by   c) in the field of

3 a) if only   b) though perhaps   c) albeit

4 a) substantiates the popular belief   b) proves the truth of what people have long believed   c) confirms what the layman has long suspected

5 a) supposed   b) said   c) known   d) thought

6 a) have more inertia   b) are more inert   c) react with greater inertia

7 a) respond to   b) move under   c) be set in motion by

8 a) act as equally opposing forces   b) are precisely counterbalanced   c) exactly cancel out

9 a) cornerstone   b) fundamental principle   c) key point

10 a) which allows them   b) enabling them   c) thus they are able

11 a) may be attributed to the fact that   b) is that   c) lies in the fact that

12 a) consequently the   b) hence   c) likewise the

KEY TO TASKS   The original expressions used by the writers are:

Task sheet A 1a   2b   3b   4c   5a   6b   7a   8b   9a   10b   11a

Task sheet B 1b   2a   3c   4c   5a   6a   7b   8c   9a   10b   11c
          12b

1.5 Transformations

PREPARATION

Basically, no material is required, as the language will be provided by the students. However, some suggestions for the kind of language expected are given under *Examples*.

IN CLASS

1 Write up a stimulus word or expression on the blackboard. This should be a short, relatively neutral statement which lends itself to transformation into different registers. Any of the following would be suitable:

- *Thank you*
- *I agree / I don't agree*
- *No smoking*
- *I'm sorry*
- *Sit down*

2 Ask the students to call out various ways of conveying the same message in different words (*Sit down*: Take a seat. / Do sit down. / Can't you find a chair? / Some of you are still standing! etc.)

For each suggestion, the students should say as precisely as possible in what context they would expect to see or hear the words (who is speaking? to whom? where are they, or where would the words be seen?).

3 In groups of three or four, they now work in the same way on two of the other stimulus phrases. Ask them to note down their suggestions in writing, and compare notes with other groups.

4 Finally, get each group to choose any one of the stimulus phrases and work through the possible transformations in the mother tongue. They may translate from their own English expressions, but should also try to add new ones appropriate to the target language (TL) (*asseyez-vous, prenez place, ne vous dérangez pas*).

COMMENTS

1 This is an exercise in register, that is, in finding language suited to the context.

In step 2 (above), the students will probably have little difficulty in offering suggestions ('Would you mind sitting down!'), but they may need to be pressed to locate the context, that is, to say when, where, and how such expressions might be used.

2 If the students do not, of their own accord, offer a context for their example, there is a simple (if crude) way of persuading them to think more precisely. Write up on the board or on an overhead projector (OHP) two columns, one headed *places* the other *people*.

For instance:

People	Places
banker	*train / bus / plane*
beggar	*courtroom*
policeman	*lift*
customs officer	*theatre*
diplomat	*lecture-hall*
film-director	*market-place*
bus-conductor	*laboratory*
shop assistant	*dentist's waiting-room*
(un)friendly neighbour	*hotel lobby (reception)*
judge	*factory*

Ask the students to choose from the two columns either a person or a place, to give a context to the remark. For example:
– *film-director* (to restless actor): 'Would you mind sitting down!'
– (air-hostess) to restless passenger *in a plane*: 'Would you mind sitting down!'

3 Although this activity involves no work on texts, it still has a direct bearing on translation. For all translation is selection: we choose from a range of possible expressions the one most appropriate to the context. Even the simplest expressions may be rendered in many different ways for example, in a business letter, the words *je vous prie de* might be translated as 'Would you kindly . . .' 'Could you please . . .' 'We would appreciate it if . . .', depending on the tone and the context. The purpose of the activity is to encourage the students to think through the possibilities. (See also activity 5.2.)

EXAMPLES

Below are examples of the kind of expressions that students might offer for the stimulus phrases.

1 *THANK YOU*

(mainly spoken)
– (I'm) most obliged.
– Thanks a lot.
– Many thanks.
– I can never repay you!
– Ta.
– I'm extremely grateful.
– How (very) kind!
– You shouldn't have . . .!
– What a lovely surprise!
– Oh, *thank* you!

(mainly written)
– Please convey our thanks to . . .
– We should like to acknowledge our thanks for/to . . .
– And in conclusion, a word of thanks to . . .
– Finally, I should like to express my gratitude to . . .
– I should like you to know how grateful I am for . . .
– It was most kind of you to . . .
– We thank you for your consideration/understanding.

2 *I DO NOT AGREE*

(mainly spoken)

- You're wrong.
- Have it your own way.
- Surely not?
- With all due respect . . .
- No. No. No!
- Nonsense! (Rubbish! etc.)

- I don't agree/I do *not* agree.
- You may have a point, but . . .
- I beg to differ . . .
- I think it would be unwise.
- Yes, but . . .
- Hmmm . . .

(mainly written)

- There are, however, certain points with which I take issue . . .
- Far be it from me to criticize, but . . .
- The mistaken assumption here is that . . .
- This is simply not so.
- The argument is fallacious in several respects.
- To such a proposal, in all conscience, I could never agree.

1.6 Odd man out

PREPARATION

1 Make up sets of words or expressions, four of which have some feature in common which is not shared by the fifth, for instance:
thoughtful   pensive   considerate   sympathetic   understanding
(The 'odd man out' is *pensive*, because it does not imply caring for others.)

2 Ensure you have enough copies of each set for one third of the class.

IN CLASS

1 Ask students to work in groups of three. Give each group one of the sets of examples in the task sheets. They should discuss which they think is the 'odd man out' in each case. Remind them that it may be possible to find two solutions, provided they can justify both.

2 When they are ready, they should exchange sets with another group, and discuss the new examples. This time each group should write down, as succinctly as possible, its reasons for choosing the 'odd man out' in each case.

3 Conduct a round-up session with the whole class. Run through the examples, asking the groups to read out their solutions. Be sure to allow time for discussion and disagreement.

COMMENTS

1 This activity will, of course, be carried out entirely in English. As an extension, however, you could ask the students to devise their own 'odd man out' tasks in their mother tongue, and then try them out on each other.

2 You will probably find that when this activity is tried out for the first time the students will tend to be content merely with identifying the 'odd man out'. But this is not the real purpose of the activity. The aim is to explain (in English) the reason for their choice. This is why it is suggested in step 2 that they write down their reasons, as writing helps to focus the discussion.

3 Devising the sets: Many of the words used in the sets are words which will recur in the texts later in this book (*allege, maintain, claim, assert, confirm*). This activity is a useful way of getting students to think about the range of meaning of words which are already familiar to them. Teachers planning to devise their own sets could draw upon the material in their own textbooks.

4 Following the task sheets, I have given the solutions I had in mind. They are, of course, not the only ones possible.

TASK SHEET A

In each of the sets of words below, one word or expression stands out as being in some way different from the others. This is the 'odd man out'. Which do you think it is, in each case, and why? When you have made your choice, discuss your reasons with your partners.

1 showery   unstable   fine   lovely   changeable
2 fine   O.K.   very well   all right   why not?
3 supersede   oust   give way to   dispense with   replace
4 objective   unbiased   indifferent   impartial   disinterested
5 pick out   discern   envisage   notice   spot

TASK SHEET B

In each of the sets of words below, one word or expression stands out as being in some way different from the others. This is the 'odd man out'. Which do you think it is, in each case, and why? When you have made your choice, discuss your reasons with your partners.

1 criminal   culprit   wrongdoer   villain   miscreant
2 find out   learn   ascertain   discover   deduce
3 a.m.   B.C.   i.e.   e.g.   A.D.   p.m.
4 malleable   expansile   ductile   fragile   pliable
5 constant   regular   steady   incessant   continuous

TASK SHEET C

In each of the sets of words below, one word or expression stands out as being in some way different from the others. This is the 'odd man out'. Which do you think it is, in each case, and why? When you have made your choice, discuss your reasons with your partners.

1 quite far   quite hard   quite right   quite interesting   quite good
2 refer to   allude to   touch upon   expound   mention
3 take   tolerate   put up with   withstand   accept
4 colossal   huge   vast   lofty   immense
5 renowned   eminent   distinguished   prestigious   well-known

TASK SHEET D

In each of the sets of words below, one word or expression stands out as being in some way different from the others. This is the 'odd man out'. Which do you think it is, in each case, and why? When you have made your choice, discuss your reasons with your partners.

1 careful   thorough   punctilious   pedantic   precise
2 shiver   shudder   shatter   tremble   shake
3 block   hinder   obstruct   impair   impede
4 kind   thoughtful   pensive   considerate   understanding
5 A stitch in time saves nine.
   A bird in the hand is worth two in the bush.
   A thing of beauty is a joy forever.
   It takes all sorts to make a world.
   If a job's worth doing, it's worth doing well.

NOTE: You may make photocopies of these for classroom use (but please note that copyright law does not normally permit multiple copying of published material).

KEY TO TASKS

Task sheet A

1 *lovely*: the only word one would not expect to hear in a radio or TV weather report.
2 *very well*: suggests reluctant accpetance, even disapproval; all the other expressions are neutral or positive.
3 *dispense with*: means to remove or do without; the other expressions all imply replacing one thing/person with another.
4 *indifferent*: means showing lack of interest rather than impartiality.

5 *envisage*: suggests planning; the other words focus on observation of detail.

Task sheet B

1 *villain*: the only word one would not expect to find in a formal legal context.

2 *deduce*: the only word which necessarily implies coming to a conclusion, or interpreting facts.

3 *B.C.*: the only non-Latin abbreviation.

4 *fragile*: means 'breakable'; all the other words refer to altering shape without breaking.

5 *incessant*: the most negative word in the group (for example, the incessant noise of traffic); the others are all neutral.

Task sheet C

1 *quite right*: means absolutely right; in the other expressions quite has the meaning of 'fairly, relatively'.

2 *expound*: the only word which implies explanation (as in 'expound a theory') rather than merely reference.

3 *withstand*: the only word which is not associated with behaviour, attitudes, ideas, etc. Unlike the other words, it could not be used in a sentence such as: 'I cannot . . . his attitude.'

4 *lofty*: the only word which is restricted to height, and cannot refer to physical expanse, extent, or bulk.

5 *prestigious*: the only word which is not associated with an individual person (though it could be used for a firm or company).

Task sheet D

1 *pedantic*: in English, this is used in a negative sense – 'fussy' or 'over-careful'; the other words are all used positively.

2 *shatter*: the other words do not imply breaking.

3 *impair*: meaning to harm, make worse or less effective (for example, the driver's vision at night may be impaired by fog or dazzling headlights); all the other words are primarily associated with physical obstruction.

4 *pensive*: because one is concerned with one's own thoughts, not with consideration of others.

5 *A thing of beauty is a joy forever*: this is the only quotation (Keats); the others are either proverbs or popular sayings.

1.7 Colloquial expressions

PREPARATION

1 Choose short passages illustrating colloquial uses of common adjectives (*little, poor, low, large, big*), and make them up into task sheets.

(The same approach might also be used for other parts of speech such as nouns, prepositions, and adverbs.)

2 Make enough copies of the task sheets so that half the pairs or groups have one task sheet, and the other half have a different one.

IN CLASS

1 As a warm-up, get the students to call out any common adjectives in English. Write these up on the board or OHP. Then ask the students to suggest any nouns that are naturally associated with the adjectives:

- *little*: hope, chance, time, room, likelihood
- *poor*: performance, result(s), grasp/understanding, quality
- *low*: intensity, opinion, standard, level, life
- *large*: amount, share, dimensions, proportions
  etc.

2 Ask the students to pick out any combinations which might be rendered differently in their own language (*of low intensity = slabog intenziteta*, that is, of 'weak' intensity).

3 Next, divide the students into pairs or groups of three. Give each group one set of examples or task sheet. The students should try to find suitable translations for the words in italics. When they are ready, they compare notes with any other pair that has worked on the same set.

4 An optional activity is for the students to discuss any difficulties they may have had with others who have worked on a different task sheet.

TASK SHEET A

Suggest suitable translations for the expressions in italics in the passages below.

1 A girl I know, who prided herself on her long slender thighs, gave up short dresses for ever after an assistant at a department store told her: 'The trouble is, Madam, *you've got low knees.*' (*The Sunday Times*)

2 Tito has shown even in old age the capacity to learn and the will to change with the times – but not too hastily or fundamentally. *It is small wonder* that this extraordinary man, who has lived through enough experience for several full lives, should have become a legend in his own lifetime.
(Phyllis Auty: *Tito: A Biography*)

3 The Indian heart of hospitality is as a rule almost limitless, but Indian *small talk is the smallest in the world.* Party conversation at a formal middle-class reception has a strange period charm, so faithfully does it parody the dafter conventions of the English scene.
(James Cameron: *An Indian Summer*)

4 The editors have aimed the book at both engineers and lay
  readers, though I think the latter would find some of it *a little
  heavy going*.
  (book review, *New Scientist*)

5 Land development in and around Birmingham has strained local
  resources to the limit. Water and electricity now have to be
  brought at *great expense* from hundreds of miles away. *Heavy
  investment* by local authorities to help develop towns and villages
  further afield is unlikely to ease the situation.
  (*The Midlands Developer*)

TASK SHEET B

Suggest suitable translations for the expressions in italics in the
passages below.

1 Before a cabinet meeting, the Minister is carefully 'briefed' for
  any set speech: for such an occasion he is supplied with full notes
  on any point likely to be raised, even with anecdotes and *'light
  relief'* of a very decorous official nature.
  (Erving Goffman: *The Presentation of Self in Everyday Life*)

2 (Dr) Johnson began by thinking that the language was divided
  into acceptable words and *low words*. For instance, he didn't like
  the noun 'scrape', meaning a difficulty ('I got into a scrape'). So
  he put it in the Dictionary grudgingly and marked it with words
  to the effect that this was a *low word* to be avoided.
  ('Rescuing Johnson from Caricature': *The Listener*)

3 The results of the test (of the quality of concrete building blocks)
  should be sent to the supervising officer. *When low results are
  obtained*, instructions must be given to improve the quality of the
  concrete mix, and, if necessary, *the poor batch* must be broken out
  and replaced.
  (J. T. Bowyer: *Small Works Supervision*)

4 If anyone is asked to rate a person, whom he knows sufficiently
  well, on a number of personality variables, he will tend to be
  influenced by his general opinion of the person. *If he has a high
  opinion* of the person he will *tend to rate him high* on all desirable
  qualities, and *vice versa if he has a low opinion*.
  (C. J. Adcock: *Fundamentals of Psychology*)

5 To a large extent, Viking ships were sailed within sight of land,
  but when ships crossed the seas to Iceland or to America, some
  form of navigational aid must have been used. The Vikings *seem
  to have had a fair idea of latitude*, but none of longitude.
  (David M. Wilson: *The Vikings*)

'I'm afraid a low interest is what I
take in *any* loan application.'

VARIATION	**Phrasal verbs**

PREPARATION

1 Collect passages illustrating common uses of phrasal verbs (*turn out, carry on, put up with*). Examples are to be found in the task sheets that follow.

2 Make up enough task sheets so that half the class (working in pairs) has one set, and the other half a different set.

3 Another alternative is to choose a much longer text (of around 60 lines) from a book or newspaper article. Try to find a text that contains a number of colloquial expressions/phrasal verbs.

IN CLASS

1 Ask the students to work in pairs. Each pair has one of the task sheets. They may translate the passages orally, but must note down in writing their rendering of the words in italics. They should suggest two translations for each of these expressions.

2 When they are ready, get each pair to exchange notes with another pair who have worked on the same task sheet. Together they should decide which translation, in each case, is best suited to the context.

3 Each pair now joins with a pair who have worked on a different task sheet. They exchange material and suggest off-the-cuff oral translations of the phrases in italics. These can then be matched against the written suggestions both pairs have for their own material.

COMMENTS

1 In both activity 1.7 and its variation, the students are working with colloquial everyday language. This means that in many cases they will come up with almost identical translations, that is, expressions such as *high opinion/low opinion* or *send out/take in* (signals), which may have more or less fixed equivalents in their mother tongue. But there will also be plenty of room for personal interpretation (*an up-and-down job*, or *he wins through*). What is particularly interesting in the discussion is the fact that some expressions are 'closed' (that is, the translations are almost predictable), while others are 'open' (unpredictable).

2 Many of the questions raised by this activity (such as choice of words) will be returned to later on in this book. Here, we are simply trying to make the student aware of the scope of even the most 'ordinary' words (*little*, *big*, *put*, *get*, etc.), and to think about why certain words are used rather than others. Why, for instance, does someone say: 'I never go around putting on toughness', and not, 'I never make a deliberate display of strength'? (See task sheet B.)

3 See also activity 5.3.

TASK SHEET A

Suggest suitable translations for all words in italics in the passages below. Wherever possible, offer two translations for each expression, and note the one which you consider better suited to the context.

1 In south India, the Madras studios, *which turn out films* in a dozen languages, have been involved since Independence in politics. (Trevor Fishlock: *India File*)

2 Some people *are always up in the clouds or down in the depths.* They swing from one extreme to another. Others are stolid and indifferent, never much thrilled by success and *never greatly put out* by failure. (C. J. Adcock: *Fundamentals of Psychology*)

3 Social behaviour is *a matter of output and input. We send out signals* with our own actions, and *we take in messages* from the actions of others. When all is well we achieve a balance between these two, but sometimes this equilibrium is upset. (Desmond Morris: *Manwatching*)

4 (Former Prime Minister) Sir Anthony Eden's main metaphor groups are sensual and related to smoothing, rubbing, stroking and eating. Molotov (he said) *'did what he could to rub off some of the sharp angles'*, but at the end of the conference they had to admit that there were matters *'that cannot be ironed out between us'*. (Kenneth Hudson: *The Language of Modern Politics*)

5 In great cities men are like a lot of stones thrown together in a bag; *their jagged corners are rubbed off* till in the end they are as smooth as marbles. (Somerset Maugham: *A Writer's Notebook*)

6 A good talker *can talk away the substance* of twenty books in as many evenings. He will describe the central idea of the book he means to write until it revolts him. (Cyril Connolly: *The Unquiet Grave*)

TASK SHEET B	Suggest suitable translations for all words in italics in the passages below. Wherever possible, offer two translations for each expression, and note the one which you consider better suited to the context.

1 A month ago, a bundle of about 70 dictionary slips was discovered in the Printing Division of the Oxford University Press. *They turned out to be* the original copy of almost the first words of the OED (Oxford English Dictionary) sent by James Murray to the printers in April 1882.
(*The Linguist*)

2 Men are prepared to go to extraordinary lengths to get political power. They will sacrifice health, comfort and domestic peace, *put up with almost unlimited amounts* of public criticism and abuse, and risk the humiliations and disappointments of defeat.
(Kenneth Hudson: *The Language of Modern Politics*)

3 **Interviewer** You often give the impression of being very tough, often pugnacious, yet some of your contemporaries seem to remember you as a very gentle person.
Edward Heath I can assure you that *I never go around putting on toughness*.
(interview with a former Prime Minister)

4 Most films (in India) have fight scenes to enable the hero to demonstrate his masculinity. Battered and bloody, *he wins through*.
(Trevor Fishlock: *India File*)

5 We nearly always eat the same thing for breakfast. This is because we are at our most insecure in the morning. When we wake, we need the reassurance of something familiar *to see us through the first moments*, and this familiarity is provided by the unvarying breakfast menu.
(Desmond Morris: *Manwatching*)

1.8 Word play

PREPARATION	1 Make a selection of ten to twelve titles (books, films, plays, etc.) and/or advertising slogans. These should be titles or slogans that can be easily understood. If you wish, add a short explanation, for instance: *Manwatching* – a book on human behaviour. The task sheet for this activity gives suitable examples.

2 Make up a similar task sheet and prepare enough copies for everyone in the class.

IN CLASS

1 Divide the students into groups of four. Ask them to imagine that the book, film, or product is to be distributed in their country. Each group should suggest translations for the titles or slogans.

2 After discussion, the groups offer their suggestions to the whole class.

COMMENTS

This is a useful warming up (or cooling down!) activity. It should be kept short, that is, to ten or fifteen minutes at the most. Ask the students to keep their eyes open for other examples which could be used in later classes.

TASK SHEET

Below is a selection of titles of books, films, TV programmes, and advertising slogans. Imagine in each case that the book, product, or programme is to be distributed in your country. Suggest how the title or slogan could be rendered in your own language. (Feel free to use your imagination.)

1 *A Taste of India*
(title of an illustrated book on Indian cooking)

2 *Manwatching*
(title of a book on human behaviour – gesture and movement)

3 Heineken – *Refreshes the parts other beers cannot reach*
(advertisement for Heineken beer)

4 Johnny Walker – *Born 1820, and still going strong*
(advertisement for Johnny Walker whisky)

5 *The Heart of the Dragon*
(title of a TV documentary series on China)

6 *Educating Rita*
(title of a film based on a stage comedy about a young hairdresser, Rita, who decides to 'improve her mind' at a summer university course, with her reluctant tutor, Frank)

7 *The Ascent of Man*
(TV documentary series tracing the development of the human race since prehistoric times)

8 *Take the Money and Run*
(title of a film – a farce, with Woody Allen as an unsuccessful crook who repeatedly ends up in jail)

9 CANADA – THE BIG COUNTRY FOR BIG VALUE HOLIDAYS
(Tourism Division of the Canadian High Commission)

2 Word order and reference

Introduction

A common excuse for incoherence is: 'I know what I want to say, but I can't seem to find the words.' As if it were somehow the fault of the words for getting lost. In fact, it is most often when we do not know what we want to say that we cannot find the words. Words do not run away.

But even when we can 'find' the words, we still have to put them in order, and that order can make a great deal of difference to what we 'want to say'. As an illustration, let me quote an anecdote told by E. E. Schumacher (in *A Guide for the Perplexed*):

> There is a story of two monks who were passionate smokers and tried to settle between themselves the question of whether it was permissible to smoke while praying. As they could not come to a conclusion they decided to ask their respective superiors. One of them got into deep trouble with his abbot; the other received a pat of encouragement. When they met again, the first one, slightly suspicious, inquired of the second: 'What did you actually ask?' and received the answer: 'I asked whether it was permissible to pray while smoking'.

What we mean is both what we say and how we say it. English is not a language noted for the flexibility of its word order. A word out of place can easily alter the meaning, or lead to ambiguity. Take these two simple examples:

> Niall Quinn, the 6ft 4in Arsenal centre-forward, *almost scored* within seconds of taking the field in the 79th minute. But the chance fizzled away off Quinn's left boot.

> Leisure parks, gardens and wildlife centres were also popular with tourists to Britain last year, while visits to museums, galleries and historic buildings slumped. One of the *worst places* affected by fewer visitors was the Royal Academy.

In the first, the word *almost* is correctly placed; if it had been shifted slightly forward, the meaning would have been quite different – 'scored *almost within minutes*'. In the second, the word *worst* should have come after *places*, not before.

But, although its word order may not be flexible, English is peculiarly elastic in its inflections, that is, in the stresses and emphases in speech and writing which help to point to the meaning.

('I like it'/'I *do* like it', 'It works'/'It *does* work'). This is a feature of the language which can easily be overlooked, particularly in writing, where the emphasis is not often marked. Yet in translation it is vital to the meaning of the sentence.

Almost half the material in this section, then, is concerned with that 'other' meaning which is conveyed through word order, stress, and emphasis. And, of course, with the closely related question of choice of words.

Paired with word order in the title is reference. This concerns mainly the 'bones' – the factual content – of the writing. What does the writer mean, what is he or she referring to, when using words such as *this, that, which, it, here*? Is it something stated, or something implied? Are there any words left out, any gaps that need to be filled (in translation)? And, perhaps most important of all, how can the same references best be made in the target language?

The question matters because it relates directly to one of the weaknesses most commonly encountered in translation, implied in the often-heard criticism: 'It doesn't sound right'. If the translation does not sound right, it is usually because the sequence of thought – and, therefore, choice of words – of the original has been too closely followed. The meaning may get through, but the style, the spirit, the way of thinking remains that of the source language. To take just one example: Consider what the effect would be if a student doggedly translated all the *it(s)* in this fragment (in which *it* refers to the Australian desert):

> Only the aborigines living in their traditional manner can survive in *it* unaided. Unlike the white man, they make no attempt to dominate *it*. They do not try to tame *its* animals or to cultivate *its* sands, but to them *it* yields enough to keep a man's soul in his body. In return, the aborigines worship *it*.

I am not, of course, suggesting that the translation could not follow the English word-for-word and yet 'sound right'. But I am suggesting that the pattern of the English should be followed only after considering the alternatives, not before.

This, then, is the common aim of all the activities: to encourage the students to think <u>from</u> English <u>into</u>, and <u>in</u>, their own language.

2.1 Stress and emphasis

PREPARATION   1 Select passages in which stress is given to certain words. This stress may be implicit in the contruction, for example:

> **Frank** Talk properly!
> **Rita**   I am talking properly.

or may be deliberately marked by the writer:

Frank You haven't got an ugly voice. At least, you *didn't* have.

In the material in the task sheets, both kinds of stress are marked in italics, with an asterisk (*) to indicate italics in the original.

2 On the blackboard write up five to ten short sentences in two forms, stressed and unstressed. For instance:

A	B
– I'm sorry.	– I *am* sorry!
– You don't remember, but I do.	– You don't remember, *but I do.*
– My son's no good at French, but he tries.	– My son's no good at French, *but he does try.*
D'you know who he is?	– D'you know who he is?
Yes, I do.	*I do indeed!*
– When do we cross the border? We've crossed the border.	– When do we cross the border? We *have* crossed the border!
– I'd like to speak to the manager.	– I'd like to speak to the manager.
I'm the manager.	*I am* the manager.

IN CLASS

1 Working as a single group, the class call out suggestions for ways in which the difference in emphasis could be brought out in translation.

2 Next, ask the students to work in groups of three, using the task sheet materials, one set to each group. They should do the translation orally, but all suggestions for the phrases in italics should be noted down.

3 Each group then joins another. They exchange sets and work separately on the new material. When they are ready, they come together again to compare translations. This will involve referring back to the notes made in step 2.

COMMENTS

1 The first task of this activity should help the students to see more clearly the difference between a stressed and an unstressed sentence.

Later, when they come to work on the task sheets (*In class*, step 2), suggest that they try to reformulate the phrases by leaving out the stress:

'I love those High Speed Trains'/'I do love those High Speed Trains.' (See task sheet B, number 3.)

This will make it easier for them to find a suitable translation.

2 Every sentence contains some kind of stress, though it may be very light. As a variation on this activity, try giving the students the material unmarked, and ask them to mark the stresses. (See also activity 2.2.)

3 Other typical stress markers are words such as: *surely, certainly, truly, undoubtedly, really, actually, obviously, absolutely, utterly,* and phrases like *It is evident that,* etc.

TASK SHEET A

In the examples below, certain words carry a particular stress. These are marked in italics. An asterisk (*) after the expression indicates that the words also appeared in italics in the original text.

Working with a partner, translate the examples orally, but note down your rendering of all words in italics.

1 *Travelling by bus does have some compensations.* It may be dusty and very, very uncomfortable. One may see only a small part of the countryside through the dirty windows, but bus travel is comparatively cheap and *one does meet people. Indeed, no one can escape,* yourself included. Everyone is united by discomfort and the excitement of the journey.
(Tim Severin: *Tracking Marco Polo*)

2 'I'm very ambitious!' she at last replied.
'And your ambitions have not been satisfied? They must have been great.'
'*They were* (*) great. I should make myself ridiculous by talking about them.'
(Henry James: *Portrait of a Lady*)

3 'Mrs Moore, what is this echo?'
'Don't you know?'
'No – what is it? *Oh, do say!*(*) I felt you would be able to explain it.'
'If you don't know, you don't know; I can't tell you.'
(E. M. Forster: *A Passage to India*)

4 No one supposes that housing estates are places where men work. Women, however, *do work there*, and for some full-time housewives it is their main place of work.
(Ronald Frankenberg: *Communities in Britain*)

5 'Have you been long in Bath, madam?'
'About a week, sir,' replied Catherine, trying not to laugh.
'Really!' with affected astonishment.
'Why should you be surprised, sir?'
'*Why, indeed!*' said he in his natural tone; 'But some emotion must appear to be raised by your reply.'
(Jane Austen: *Northanger Abbey*)

6 Are we to assume that evolution has produced in the heads of chimpanzees brains whose power far outstrips the use to which they are put? *That indeed would be a waste,* and *indeed it would be uncharacteristic of* the usually economic forces of evolution.
(Richard Leakey and Roger Lewin: *People of the Lake*)

TASK SHEET B

In the examples below, certain words carry a particular stress. These are marked in italics.

Working with a partner, translate the examples orally, but note down your rendering of all words in italics.

1 I am like the Tiger: if I miss the first spring, I go growling back to my Jungle again; but *if I do hit*, it is crushing.
(Lord Byron in a letter)

2 Somers' thoughts wandered out to the gently darkening sea, and the whole of vast Australia lying behind him flat and open to the sky.
'You like it down here?' said Jack.
'*I do indeed.*'
(D. H. Lawrence: *Kangaroo*)

3 '*I do love those High Speed Trains.* I mean, they simply waft you from one city to another. And as an actress, trains are vital to my working life.'
(Fenella Fielding in a British Rail brochure)

4 'Ah, dear mother, one always knows what to expect of *you*(*)! You've never surprised me but once, and that's today – in presenting me with a pretty cousin whose existence I had never suspected.'
'Do you think her *so very pretty?*'
'*Very pretty indeed*; but I don't insist upon that.'
(Henry James: *Portrait of a Lady*)

5 Jokingly, Hill called out to his companions, 'Look, I've found some fossilized footprints.' But it turned out to be no joke. *They were* (*) fossilized footprints.
(Richard Leakey and Roger Lewin: *People of the Lake*)

6 **Rita** (talking in a peculiar voice) Hello, Frank.
Frank (without looking up) Hello. Rita, you're late.
Rita I know, Frank. I'm terribly sorry. It was unavoidable.
Frank (looking up) Was it really? What's wrong with your voice?
Rita Nothing is wrong with it, Frank. I have merely decided to talk properly. As Trish says, there is not a lot of point in discussing beautiful literature in an ugly voice.
Frank You haven't got an ugly voice; at least, *you didn't*(*) have. Talk properly.
Rita *I am talking properly.*
Frank Rita! Just be yourself.
Rita (reverting to her normal voice) *I am being myself.*
(Willy Russell: *Educating Rita*)

2.2 Word order: opening words

1 Choose passages in which the word order of the sentences is strongly determined by the opening words. Some of the commonest of these words are: *To, That, How, Whether, Why, Where, Always, Never,* and also adjectives and personal names.

The sentences chosen should illustrate inverted word order, that is, a reversal of the normal order, as in:
– *To Wentworth*, therefore, the King turned.
  (The King therefore turned to Wentworth.)
– *Where* they had come from it was impossible to guess.
  (It was impossible to guess where they had come from.)
2 Prepare several sets of examples, such as those given in task sheets A and B, and make enough copies of each set for half the class.

1 As a preliminary task, write up one or two typical examples and ask the students to suggest how the same thoughts might be reworded in English:
– *That the Vikings discovered America is accepted by all but a few scholars.*
– It is accepted by all but a few scholars that . . .
– All but a few scholars accept the fact that . . .
– The discovery of America by the Vikings is a fact accepted by . . .

2 Ask the students to work in pairs, and give one task sheet to each pair. For each sentence with a marked opening word they should suggest, if possible, two translations, one closely matching the English word order, the other free.

3 When they are ready, they compare notes with another pair working on the same set. After discussion, each group of four chooses the translation most preferred for each example.

4 Round up the discussion by asking the groups to read out their chosen translations to the rest of the class. Also indicate your own preference, with comments or alternative suggestions.

5 If time permits, the activity can be repeated with each pair working on a new task sheet. Otherwise, the remaining sets can be given for out-of-class written work.

1 Perhaps the most important question raised by this activity is: How much does word order influence our understanding? Is the writer suggesting a particular stress which should come through in the translation? And where does that stress fall – is it necessarily at the beginning? Compare:
– *Robespierre* I find difficult to admire.
– Of all the vices to which my colleagues are most opposed, none is more hateful than *hypocrisy*.

2 There is no need, I feel, to draw the students' attention to this relation between stress and word order. With advanced groups, however, it would be interesting – after the first task has been done – to go back over the material, asking them to mark which word(s) they feel take the strongest stress in the sentence.

3 For further work along similar lines, see also activities 1.3 and 2.1.

4 Finding further material: Inverted word order is not just a literary device. It frequently occurs both in technical literature and in non-fictional prose. Sentences suitable for this activity will often be found at the beginning or end of a paragraph. If you are looking for literary examples you may find ideas in the 'Index of First Lines' of poetry anthologies, under words such as *who, what, where, how,* or *far, long, deep, slow, cold* ('Cold is the grave wherein my love is laid'). Consider also book titles such as: *Tender is the Night, How Green was My Valley, Quiet Flows the Don.*

TASK SHEET A

In each of the passages below, the opening words of certain sentences are marked in italics. Translate these sentences in whatever seems the most natural way in your own language. You do not necessarily have to begin with the same word as is used in the English.

Wherever possible, offer two translations, using different word order. But if you feel there is only one correct word order, offer only one translation.

1 *That* the Vikings discovered America is accepted by all but a few scholars who insist that Irish priests got there before them.
(David M. Wilson: *The Vikings*)

2 *So colossal is* human egotism that people who have met an author are constantly on the look-out for portraits of themselves in his work.
(Somerset Maugham: *A Writer's Notebook*)

3 From the spring of 1665 the Great Plague had raged in London. *Never* since the Black Death in 1348 had pestilence spread such ravages.
(Winston Churchill: *A History of the English Speaking Peoples*)

4 *Uneasy lies the head* that wears a crown.
(William Shakespeare: *King Henry V*)

5 *'To these islands'* (The Maldives), wrote the Arab geographer Idrisi in the twelfth century, 'come the ships of Oman to gather coconuts and cut wood and build their vessels.'
(Tim Severin: *The Sindbad Voyage*)

6 Can one say that anyone, any single figure, characterized the Jacobins? *That* the Jacobins provided the revolutionary drive and

force is indisputable, but the Jacobins themselves differed a good deal. *Marat* was a man of violent revolutionary character. *Danton*, who had been a man of violence at the time of the massacre, was anxious to go back to an easier life. *Robespierre* I find difficult to admire. It is impossible to feel any greatness in him, and yet, because of his passionate faith in the principles of the revolution, he was more representative than anyone else.
(A. J. P. Taylor in *The Listener*)

TASK SHEET B

In each of the passages below, the opening words of certain sentences are marked in italics. Translate these sentences in whatever seems the most natural way in your own language. You do not necessarily have to begin with the same word as is used in the English.

Wherever possible, offer two translations, using different word order. But if you feel there is only one correct word order, offer only one translation.

1 *That* translation no longer enjoys anything like the status in foreign language teaching which it once did must be clear to anyone.
   (*The Linguist*)

2 *Wentworth* was the man of all others most worth winning. His abilities were obviously of the first order, and so were his ambitions. *To Wentworth* therefore the King turned.
   (Winston Churchill: *A History of the English Speaking Peoples*)

3 *Of all the vices* to which my colleagues in journalism are most opposed, none is more hateful to them than hypocrisy. *Diligently* they seek it out in high places, always looking for politicians, bishops, and judges whose practice does not come up to their principles.
   (*The Times*)

4 *Small as she was*, she made quite a good horsewoman.
   (D. H. Lawrence: *The Princess and Other Stories*)

5 *Important though language is*, both as a channel of communication and as equipment for thinking, the really special feature of the human brain is its use of language to question our place in nature. Intense intellectual curiosity is a hallmark of mankind.
   (Richard Leakey and Roger Lewin: *People of the Lake*)

6 Since 1781, Salomon had been well established in London as a soloist and leader of an orchestra. His admiration for Haydn was well known. *Always impetuous and forceful,* he is said to have introduced himself to the composer by saying: 'My name is Salomon; I have come from London to fetch you.'
   (Neil Butterworth: *Haydn: His Life and Times*)

2.3 Reformulation and repetition

1 For this activity you will need to find passages in which the writer expresses the same thought in different words (synonyms and close equivalents), or in which the same words are repeated. For instance:

> *Rainfall* is not the simple *deluge of water drops* that it appears; the latest contributory factor to *precipitation* is a selection of marine plants . . .

2 Prepare one set of examples for each student in the class.

3 Give the students the material to work on in their own time out of class.

1 Working in groups of three or four, the students discuss their different versions.

2 When they have finished, hold a round-up session to compare points of agreement and disagreement.

3 If written preparation is not possible, divide the class into groups of three. Each group works on one set of examples, suggesting translations for all the words and phrases in italics, and noting these down. (Any surrounding text may be translated orally.)

4 After twelve to fifteen minutes, ask each group to select the passage which gave them most difficulty. Present these passages to the whole class, and call for suggestions.

1 The underlying questions here are: Why did the writer use different words or why sometimes the very same words? Was the change made merely to avoid repetition, as in: 'Not only did the train *arrive*, but it *got in* only about an hour late.' Or was it made to point out an important distinction, as between *manslaughter* and *murder*?

These questions do not need to be answered directly. The answers will come through in the students' translations.

2 In the choice of examples, I have deliberately avoided drawing on material which might be too technical for the average language student, that is, for the student whose main interest is language, not science or technology. But it is, in fact, technical language which is most suitable for this kind of activity, because of the importance placed on precise distinctions and clear formulations.

Teachers of English for Specific Purposes (ESP) in particular should find no lack of examples of reformulation in their own textbooks.

3 The questions raised here will be reconsidered, with a slight shift of emphasis, in activity 4.2. The two activities should be seen as complementary.

TASK SHEET A

In the passages below, you will find examples of the use of:
- synonym: the same thought expressed in different words, for example, *forced/compelled*
- close equivalents
- paraphrase and idiomatic association: *ductility, malleability/easily cut and shaped*, or *do not register/quite without effect*
- repetition: the same word, though not necessarily in the same form, such as *impaired/impairment*.

These features are all marked in the text. Translate the passages, paying particular attention to the words in italics.

1 My new home was *nondescript*, in the strict sense of there being *nothing to describe*. Wallpaper, carpets, and furniture had all been chosen so as to defeat memory.
(Clive James: *Unreliable Memoirs*)

2 Eyes can be *impaired* by a number of *diseases*. Some of *these* affect only the eye; in *others*, the *impairment* of the eye is a symptom of *disease* in some other parts of the body – in the kidneys, for example.
(Aldous Huxley: *The Art of Seeing*)

3 It should be noted that, although our senses are *sensitive to* a considerable range of stimuli, we have evidence for the existence of stimuli which *do not register on them.* The electrical waves propagated by radio stations are *quite without effect on us* until converted into sound by our radio receiver.
(C. J. Adcock: *Fundamentals of Psychology*)

4 Lead is the softest of the common metals and has a high degree of *ductility, malleability*, and *resistance to corrosion.* The material is *easily cut and shaped* and does not appreciably work-harden. Lead is very *resistant to* town, country, and marine *exposure*, the bright metal being tarnished by atmospheric action to produce a fine grey film on the surface which protects the underlying metal.
(J. T. Bowyer: *Small Works Supervision*)

5 Judges frequently say, when they give their reasons for passing a sentence, that they have been *driven*, or *compelled*, or *forced* to come to a particular conclusion, *sometimes* without difficulty, *sometimes* with regret, *sometimes* with considerable *doubt or hesitation*; only to hear their colleagues announce that they have been *driven, compelled, forced* down a *different* road to a *different* conclusion.
(The Reith Lectures, *The Listener*)

TASK SHEET B

In the passages below, you will find examples of the use of:
- synonym: the same thought expressed in different words, for example *arrive / get in*
- close equivalents: *deceit / feigning*
- repetition: the same word, though not necessarily in the same form, as in *good / good*

These features are all marked in the text. Translate the passages, paying particular attention to the words in italics.

1 A man with average, or less than average, intelligence *may set his heart on* being a doctor, or a girl with little more than average looks and no acting ability *may aspire to* Hollywood stardom. The results can easily be disastrous.
(C. J. Adcock: *Fundamentals of Psychology*)

2 Though most people would agree that *incoherence, illogicality,* and *irrationality* would be serious defects in a law, few would say that the law was good just because it was *coherent, logical,* and *based on a clear principle.* Judges will very properly aim for these qualities. But in themselves, even when achieved, they do not make the law *good.* The law can be considered *good* only if, being *coherent, predictable,* and *principled,* it also produces results which are socially acceptable.
(The Reith Lectures, *The Listener*)

3 Early next morning the train *arrived*, to my mind miraculously, in Moscow. *Not only did it arrive*, but *it got in* only about an hour late, which, someone informed me, was quite unprecedented.
(Noel Coward: *Memoirs*)

4 The expressiveness of the individual, and therefore his capacity to *give impressions*, appears to involve two radically different kinds of sign activity: the expression that he *gives* and the expression that he *gives off.* The first involves verbal symbols which he uses solely to convey information . . . The second involves a wide range of action that others can treat as symptomatic of the actor. As we shall see, this distinction has only an initial validity. The individual does of course intentionally *convey* misinformation by means of both of these types of communication, the first involving *deceit*, the second *feigning.* Of the two types of communication – expressions *given* and expressions *given off* – this report will be primarily concerned with the latter.
(Erving Goffman: *The Presentation of Self in Everyday Life*)

2.4 Articles

PREPARATION

1 Find short passages illustrating various uses of the articles (*a* and *the*) and of *one* in English. And also of the missing or 'zero' article (ø). Your selection should range from standard uses (*over (ø) lunch, for a week*), to colloquial and semi-idiomatic uses (are you still *doing the writing?*).

2 Prepare two sets of task sheets and make enough copies for the whole class.

IN CLASS

1 In preparation for this activity, ask the students to call out any titles (of books, songs, films, etc.) which contain articles or in which the article is missing:

- *The Heart of Darkness*
- *West Side Story*
- *A Man for All Seasons*
- *Man Against Nature*

- *The Agony and the Ecstasy*
- *Cry, the Beloved Country*
- *A Month in the Country*
- *The Third Man*

(See also activity 1.8.)

Call for translations of each title and discuss those which differ most from the English.

2 Hand out the task sheets and ask the students to work on either of them in groups of three. They should translate each passage orally, noting down all suggested translations of the words in italics, and then compare notes with others who have worked on the same task sheet.

3 When the students have finished working on one task sheet, ask them to look at the second, and to call out any passages with which they have difficulty. The other students suggest solutions.

COMMENTS

1 The central question of this activity is the different ways of expressing the English article in the L1. This is particularly important with regard to languages with no article (Serbo-Croatian), or with article usage seemingly similar to English (French, Hungarian).

The written language sets the pattern of our thoughts. When an article occurs, our natural reaction is to translate it, whether it is needed or not.

2 A useful way of illustrating the difference between English and the L1 in the use of articles is to give the students short passages (from travel brochures, etc.) which have already been translated from English into the L1 for them to translate back into English and to compare with the original texts. (See also activity 5.2 and 5.6.)

3 Although it is not possible to explore the special uses of the article here, examples may be found in recipes, instructions, legal documents, regulations, etc.

TASK SHEET A

The passages below illustrate some common uses of the articles in English. These include the definite and indefinite articles, *the* and *a*, the missing or 'zero' article (ø), and the use of *one* as a substitute article.

Translate the passages in whatever seems the most natural way in your own language. Remember that articles can often be transformed into adjectival expressions. For example, *the heat of the day* might, in translation, become 'the midday heat'.

1 *The land* around Alice Springs seems as lifeless as any desert, during *the heat of the day*. Most of *the animals* that live here hide away from *the assault of the sun*. *A few birds* can withstand it, and one or two reptiles positively relish it.
(David Attenborough: *Journeys to the Past*)

2 Today, when *a girl* says she is going to be independent, it means she is going to devote her attentions almost exclusively to (ø) *men*; though not necessarily to '*a man*'.
(D. H. Lawrence: *The Princess and Other Stories*)

3 To flatter myself that I had something important to do in Veracruz I made *a list of* (ø) *provisions* that I intended to buy for my trip to Guatemala. Then I remembered *I had no ticket*. I went immediately to the railway station. 'I cannot sell you *a ticket* today,' said *the man* at *the window*.
'When can I buy *one*?'
'When are you leaving?'
'Thursday.'
'Fine. I can *sell you one* Thursday.'
'Why can't I *buy one* today?'
'It is not done.'
'What if there are no seats on Thursday?'
He laughed. 'On that train there are always seats.'
(Paul Theroux: *The Old Patagonian Express*)

4 Many years ago I bought (for a shilling) a two-volume, leather-bound, early eighteenth-century collection of French poetry in a junk shop. When I showed it recently to an antiquarian book dealer, he told me it was *a sensational find*. I knew, of course, that it was *an early edition*, but I hadn't realized *its* full significance. It seems what I had was *the* first edition . . .
(*The Antiquarian*)

5 *Over* (ø) *lunch* in Trujillo we discussed the lack of any adequate protection for *the monuments* we had seen *during the morning* . . . Lima lies in the tropics, but *the morning* into which we stepped was as bleakly untropical as *a Glasgow dawn*.
(George Woodcock: *Incas and Other Men*)

TASK SHEET B

The passages below illustrate some common uses of the article in English. These include the definite and indefinite articles, *the* and *a*, the missing, or 'zero' article (ø), and the use of *one* as a substitute article.

Translate the passages in whatever seems the most natural way in your language. Remember that adjectival expressions in English may need to be transformed in other languages. For example, *the glass surfaces* might, in translation, become 'the surfaces of glass'.

1 If *a housewife* is concerned with showing that she maintains cleanliness standards, she is likely to focus *her attention* upon *the glass surfaces* in her living-room, for (ø) *glass shows dirt* all too clearly; she will give less attention to *the darker* and less revealing *rug*, which may well have been chosen *in the belief* that '(ø) *dark colours* do not show *the dirt.*'
(Erving Goffmann: *The Presentation of Self in Everyday Life*)

2 My mother was worried by my bony appearance. Noticing I had not brought pajamas *for the night*, she thought I must be *short of* (ø) *money*. She looked at me with suspicion: 'Are you still *doing the writing*?' She always spoke of it as if (ø) *writing* were some unlucky thing – like (ø) *rain* – and that I was out in it without a coat.
(V. S. Pritchett: *Midnight Oil*)

3 Winston Churchill was one of *the few people* to *get the better of the playwright*, George Bernard Shaw. Shaw invited Churchill to *the first night* of his play, enclosing two tickets: 'One for yourself and one for *a friend – if you have one.*' Churchill wrote back, saying he couldn't make it, but asking if he could have tickets for the second night – '*if there is one*'.
(quoted in an advertisement for Epson computers)

4 (ø) *Light* is reflected in a different manner by shiny surfaces, or by dull or matt surfaces, and this affects the appearance of *the colour*.
(M. D. Vernon: *The Psychology of Perception*)

5 **Britain Falls Foul of Water Clean-up Bid**

Britain has told the European Commision that *the country* cannot cut chemical pollution in (ø) *drinking water* in line with *a directive* that has been in force for two years. It wants standards *in the directive* relaxed to allow more pollution *in the water*. The directive lays down that no drinking water should contain more than 50 mg of nitrate per litre at any time. But, by some estimates, up to 50 million people in Britain receive (ø) *water* that breaks *the limit*.
(*The Observer*)

2.5 Compounds

PREPARATION

1 Make a selection of short passages containing compounds such as: *long-term, hard-earned, far-reaching, drought-stricken.* Some will be hyphenated (*high-rise*), while others will consist of single words (*screwdriver, input*) or separate words (*guest list, delivery date*).

2 Make up two sets of task sheets for half the class.

IN CLASS

1 On the blackboard or OHP, write up a number of words which commonly form part of Englsh compounds:

self–	*–free*
full–	*–resistant*
open–	*–proof*
far–/high–/wide–/low–	*–based*
new–/newly–/old–/	*–rate/–capacity*
hard–/soft–	*–made/–grown*
long–/short–	*–rooted/–seated*
light–/heavy–	*–away/–off/–up*
etc.	

2 Ask the class to suggest any English compounds containing words from either column (birth-*rate*, *far*-reaching, water*proof*). For each suggestion, the students should offer a translation in their own language. (Following *Comments* is a short list of compounds which might be suggested.)

3 Get the students to work in pairs.

4 Give out task sheet A to half the class, and task sheet B to the other half, and ask the students to work orally on their task sheet. However, the translation of the expressions in italics should be noted down.

5 When each pair is ready, they should exchange task sheets with another pair, and discuss and compare their notes.

FOLLOW-UP

If English-language newspapers are available, ask the students to scan a few pages each and pick out any compounds which they would consider challenging for translation into the L1. Later, in class, each student could present two or three examples, and invite the others to suggest translations.

COMMENTS

Compound expressions abound in English, and, because they are so deeply rooted in the structure of the language, they can prove frustratingly difficult to translate. Generally, the problem is not so much understanding what is meant as finding a suitably concise expression in the L1. How does one translate, for instance, *high-rise apartments for low-income families*, or *MANTOOL: a recently-established, Manchester-based, precision-tool manufacturing company*?

Possible compounds: Overleaf I have listed a number of compounds that might be suggested in the introductory task.

- *short- / long-term credit*
- *water-based paints*
- *wide-angle lens*
- *newly-opened supermarket*
- *far-reaching consequences*
- *custom-built car*
- *fireproof lining*
- *rust-proof paint*

- *hard-wearing fabrics*
- *self-appointed spokesman*
- *self-centred attitude*
- *duty-free shop*
- *fold-back seats*
- *open-door policy*
- *pollution-free river*
- *hard-won earnings*

TASK SHEET A   Translate the following sentences orally, but note down the translation of the expressions given in italics.

1 Noise levels at the Austerlitz *rail terminus*, Paris, have been greatly reduced by the application of *sound-absorbing* tiles of synthetic rubber. The tiles are *oil–resistant, fire-resistant*, and flexible enough to be applied on uneven concrete surfaces. (*New Scientist*)

2 We knew him vaguely. He was usually invited to our embassy parties. He was, somehow, on the *permanent guest list*. But he was seldom a guest. I had seen him once, but only long enough to shake his hand – a damp, slack, *small-boned hand*. The only other thing that I could remember was that he had been wearing *evening-dress of an old-fashioned kind*. He looked uncomfortable in this stiff and slightly *ill-fitting suit*, and it also looked forty years *out of date*. (Paul Theroux: *The London Embassy*)

3 The Lewis Law: If your *outgo* exceeds your *income*, your *upkeep* will be your *downfall*. (John Peers: *1001 Logical Laws*)

4 (In a job interview) the interviewer will often have to make decisions of *far-reaching importance* for the interviewee, on the sole basis of information gained from the applicant's *interview-performance*. (Erving Goffmann: *The Presentation of Self in Everyday Life*)

5 Fijians are tall and *big-boned*, but Tongans – if the 'Tasi's' captain and crew were anything to go by – are big in a different way: big all round, verging on the corpulent. In his way, the captain reminded me of a very genial Japanese 'sumo' wrestler. 'We will be very happy to take you,' he said, beaming. 'Everyone here will be happy with you! They like to talk.' He wore a 'Hawaiian' shirt of delicate *sea-blues and sea-greens*, pinks and yellows, over a long blue kilt: *a many-splendoured Buddha* with *close-cropped white hair* and eyes that, when he smiled, were pinched up *Mongol-fashion* by his billowing cheeks. (Gavin Young: *Slow Boats Home*)

TASK SHEET B   Translate the following sentences orally, but note down the expressions given in italics.

1 Outwardly the lion society, based on the 'pride' of a couple of males, a few females, and 60 per cent cubs, is a model of order and peace. The members are forever *head-rubbing* to cement their alliance. The males form *life-long friendships*, doing battle as a team, and peaceably swopping the females. The lionesses co-operate in hunting and *in cub-rearing*.
(*New Scientist*)

2 Nehru *half-jestingly* called himself the first English prime minister of India.
(Trevor Fishlock: *India File*)

3 The site of the factory is *low-lying* with a high *water table*, and lies below the *high-tide level* of the Thames. The *sub-soil* is of poor *load-bearing capacity* with an *underlying stratum* of peat of varying thickness.
(*Architectural Design*)

4 Farmers (in Ethiopia) are to be given greater freedom to sell any additional surplus to the highest bidder, and the Government plans to establish a system of licensed *free-market traders* in order to move crops from the areas of surplus to *drought-affected regions* more easily.
(*The Farmer's Gazette*)

5 I walked towards Pevensey (Pevensey Bay being the spot where William landed his army in 1066) and decided that anyone who came ashore at Cooden Beach would find himself face to face with the quintessential England – not just coastal, *seaside holiday*, retirement England, but secretive, *rose-growing*, *dog-loving*, *window-washing*, *church-going*, *law-abiding*, grumpy, *library-using*, *tea-drinking*, fussy and inflexible England.
(Paul Theroux: *The Kingdom by the Sea*)

6 In the southeast corner of Botswana, lies the town of Lobatse, the country's main *cattle centre*. The pride of Lobatse is its abattoir, the biggest *beef factory* in Africa. Every day, within its gleaming and sterile interior, 1800 cattle are slaughtered and processed with *conveyor-belt efficiency*. The Lobatse slaughterhouse is the *flagship* of the *government-owned* Botswana Meat Corporation (BMC), and the only abattoir in the country. The *cattle business* is still the country's main employer and second biggest *foreign currency earner*. Only a fraction of Botswana's beef is used to feed its own people – more than half of whom are receiving *food aid* from the USA. The rest is exported. 'European chefs know all about prime Botswana meat,' boasts a *full page advertisement* on the cover of Air Botswana's *in-flight magazine*.
(*The Sunday Times*)

2.6 Reference and meaning

1 Choose short passages which illustrate the use of *referential words*, that is, words which stand for something already said, or implied, in the text. Some of the commonest of these are: *it, that, this, which, these, those*.

Some examples could also include impersonal constructions with *it* (sometimes known as 'the dummy subject') where *it* is not referential: *It is known that, it may be inferred that, it is commonly believed/often said/generally thought that* . . .

2 Prepare two sets of task sheets (A and B) for half the class.

3 An alternative task is to give the students a longer text to work on in writing at home, and to use their translations as a basis for class discussion. (See task sheet C in which the main focus is on the use of the word *it*.)

1 Since the aim of this activity is to encourage precision in reference, you could begin with a warm-up task. Ask the students to consider sentences in which the references are not immediately clear, or in which there is some ambiguity. For instance:
- Conservatives, unlike their opponents, welcome opposition *which* is good for the democratic system.
- Peking's *proposals* look reasonable enough today, but there can be no guarantee *it* will stick to them after sovereignty is transferred.
- The Government makes little effort to tap European Community Funds for training women because *they* discriminate against men, according to the Department of Employment.

(Further examples can be found in activity 5.1.)

2 Ask the students to work on one of the task sheets in pairs or groups of three. They should produce oral translations for each passage, paying particular attention to the way in which they render the words in italics, and noting them down.

3 When ready, they compare translations with a group which has worked with the same task sheet.

4 As a round-up, ask each group to give an example of one difficulty they encountered. The whole class then attempts to solve the problem orally.

1 Even trained translators can find themselves trapped by the wording of the original text. That is, they follow the line of words rather than the line of thought. The result is a distorted translation, as in the following example:

> Thanks to its experience, modernly equipped plants and expert staff this electronics firm satisfies the needs of both home and foreign buyers. Its appearance on the world market and ever more firm business arrangements it concludes thanks to capital investment make it ever more prominent.

2 In this exercise, there are two questions we would like the students to be asking:

a. What precisely is meant by the words in italics (*it, that, those,* etc.)?

b. Do I need to use the same words in the translation, or are there other possibilities? Are all the *it's* and *that's* necessary?

A referential word can often stand for a whole spoken or unspoken thought. For example, in task sheet A, number 2, '*It has long been noticed* that people differ very much in their capacity to handle words and *this* is not necessarily related to their intelligence', *this* stands for 'the difference in people's capacity to handle words'. Will it be clear if *this* is translated by its closest and shortest equivalent (*ceci, esto,* etc.)?

3 The idiomatic and fixed expressions *make it, bear this out, do it in style,* are in a sense distractors. Their function is to prevent the student from looking at words such as *it* or *this* in isolation, and to be able to interpret them both literally and idiomatically.

TASK SHEET A

Look carefully at the words in italics in the passages below (particularly *it, this, these*). In most cases, these words simply refer back to something already said, for example:

> Success. I don't believe *it* has any effect on me.

But in other cases they may form part of a fixed expression, as in: *It has long been noticed that . . .,* or an idiomatic expression like *What's it all about?*

Decide in each case what would be the most appropriate way of translating the words in italics. Is the *it* always needed? Is it clear what *it* means, or refers to? Could other words be used?

1 Success. I don't believe *it* has any effect on me. For one thing I always expected *it,* and *when it came I accepted it as so natural* that I didn't see anything to make a fuss about. *Its* only net value to me is that *it has freed me* from financial uncertainties. (Somerset Maugham: *A Writer's Notebook*)

2 *It has long been noticed* that people differ very much in their capacity to handle words and *this* is not necessarily related to their intelligence. (H. J. Eysenck: *Check Your Own IQ*)

3 The Venice-Simplon Orient-Express is one of the world's great railways – *not only does it get there,* but *it does it in style.* (advertisement for the Orient Express)

4 Despite his gratitude for his friendly reception *there,* Freud did not go away with a very favourable impression of America. Such prejudices were very apt to last with him, and *this one* never entirely disappeared; *it was years* before close contact with

Americans visiting Vienna *even softened it.*
(Ernest Jones: *The Life and Work of Sigmund Freud*)

5 'I think you'd better accept, dear . . . I think we'd better cable "Accept" . . . Shall I send the cablegram?'
'*Send it!*' he blurted.
She went out *and sent it.*
(D. H. Lawrence: *The Princess and Other Stories*)

6 Sir,
My husband, T. S. Eliot, loved to recount how late one evening he stopped a taxi. As he got in, the driver said: 'You're T. S. Eliot'. When asked how he knew, he replied: 'Ah. I've got an eye for a celebrity. Only the other evening I picked up Bertrand Russell and I said to him: "Well, Lord Russell, *what's it all about?*" – and, do you know, he couldn't tell me.'
(Valerie Eliot, letter to *The Times*)

TASK SHEET B

Look carefully at the words in italics in the passages below (particularly *it, this, these*). In most cases, these words simply refer back to something already said, for example: ' . . . if society wishes to show you its contempt, *it* . . . But in other cases, they may form part of a fixed expression, as in: *It has been said that* . . . . or an idiomatic expression like *What's it all about?*

Decide in each case what would be the most appropriate way of translating the words in italics. Is the *it* always needed? Is it clear what *it* means, or refers to? Could other words be used?

1 Disinterest Signals

It has been said that if society wishes to show you *its* contempt, *it* first ignores you, then if *this* does not succeed, *it* laughs at you, and finally, if all else fails, *it* attacks you. Although *this* is an oversimplification, *it is true that* the mildest, most negative form of insult is a show of disinterest.
(Desmond Morris: *Manwatching*)

2 *It is worth noticing* that children who are most punished are often the most disobedient. *It may be* that they are punished because they *are* (*) disobedient, but careful study does not seem *to bear this out.*
(C. J. Adcock: *Fundamentals of Psychology*)

3 'You must make arrangements against flies; *that* is why you are my servant,' said Aziz gently. 'Now, what have you to do?'
'Kill flies.'
'Good. *Do it.*'
(E. M. Forster: *A Passage to India*)

4 **Frank** Where's your essay?
  Rita I haven't got *it*.
  Frank You haven't done *it*?
  Rita I said I haven't got *it*.
  Frank You've lost *it*?
  Rita *It's burnt*.
  Frank Burnt?
  Rita So are all the Chekov books you lent me.
  (Willy Russell: *Educating Rita*)

5 Of all the people who have '*made it*' in Bombay none has done so more notably than the Parsees, whose ancestors fled Persia . . . and made their way across the Arabian Sea to India. Most live in and around Bombay and are uniquely bound up with *its* history, *having done for it* what Scottish businessmen did for Culcutta.
(Trevor Fishlock: *India File*)

6 – *Some Like It Hot*   (title of a film, with Marilyn Monroe)
  – *As You Like It*   (title of a play, by William Shakespeare)
  – *Take it or leave it.*   (popular expression)

TASK SHEET C

In translating the passage below, concentrate in particular on the various ways of rendering *it* and *its*.

End of the Journey

Our journey was at an end, our return to London overdue. By the time we had driven back to Alice Springs, our car could go no further. Racked and pounded by the desert, *it* could not tackle another thousand miles back to Darwin. We left *it* in a garage to be sent back to Darwin on a land-train.

We ourselves had to fly back. Below us lay the Northern Territory, the Stuart Highway a thin line scratched on *its* surface. Men had given their lives trying to explore this country. Planters and pastoralists had tried to dominate *it* and had failed. Prospectors had died trying to rifle *it* of *its* minerals. Jack Mulholland and the other men at Borroloola had come to hide themselves in *its* loneliness. But only the aborigines living in their traditional manner can survive in *it* unaided. Unlike the white man, they make no attempt to dominate *it*. They do not try to tame *its* animals or to cultivate *its* sands, but to them *it* yields enough to keep a man's soul in his body. In return, the aborigines worship *it*. *Its* rocks and *its* water-holes are the creations of their gods and their walkabouts through *it* become pilgrimages. Perhaps no one else can ever understand *it* as they do, accepting equally *its* beauty and brutality.
(David Attenborough: *Journeys to the Past*)

2.7 Short cuts: contractions and substitutes

1 Find passages in which words are omitted because the meaning is 'understood', that is, the full construction is not required to complete the sense. For instance:

'Can you state it in simple language? *If so, do.*'

Or look out for sentences in which substitute words are used in order to avoid repetition:

'But speaking out may get you into trouble.'
'It's often *done so* in the past.'

2 Prepare enough sets of task sheets A and B for the whole class.

1 Suggest the students work in pairs, and give one task sheet to each. Before translating, they should work out orally (in English) what words are missing from the expressions in italics.

2 After discussion, they write down their translations for all sentences with words in italics, and note any alternatives.

3 The students then compare and discuss with pairs who have worked on the same task sheet.

4 (Optional) Each pair joins with one which has used a different task sheet. In turn, they offer oral translations of each other's examples. They then compare them with the written translations from the other pair.

1 This activity is deceptively easy. Students will be tempted to offer the first translation that comes to mind, without checking whether it matches the underlying structure. This is why, in step 1, they are asked to complete the unspoken phrases in English. For example, in task sheet A, number 3, *Do they?* must be linked back to the words 'feel pride in a homeland called Europe'.

2 What should emerge in the discussion is that there are often several equally good ways of translating these elliptical constructions, or 'short cuts'; also, that similar expressions: *for so doing, in doing so* may be translated in quite different ways, depending on the context. It has been noted that translation into English is often shorter – by as much as ten per cent or more – than from English into most other languages. An interesting class discussion exercise would be to present the students with texts translated from English into L1 together with the original, and ask them to pick out those features of the English which were most difficult to render concisely in L1. They could then pool their observations and look for any patterns that emerge.

3 This activity is closely linked to activity 2.6.

TASK SHEET A

For the sake of brevity, or to avoid repetition, writers and speakers often leave out what is 'understood'. They may also use substitute expressions to refer to something already mentioned. For instance:

'Speaking out may get you into trouble.'
'It's often *done so* in the past.'

Here, *done so* is a substitute for 'got me into trouble'.

Working with a partner, suggest translations for all expressions in italics in your task sheet. Wherever possible, offer alternatives.

1 'But speaking out may get you into trouble.'
   '*It's often done so in the past.*'
   'There, listen to that! But the end of it might be that you lost your job.'
   '*If I do, I do.* I shall survive it.'
   (E. M. Forster: *A Passage to India*)

2 The recent use of 'psychodrama' as a therapeutic technique illustrates a further point. In these psychiatrically staged scenes patients not only act out parts with some effectiveness, but employ no script *in doing so*.
   (Erving Goffmann: *The Presentation of Self in Everyday Life*)

3 After the formation of the EEC, particularly when Britain joined the Common Market in 1972, it was hoped that our youth would feel pride in a homeland called Europe. *Do they*?
   (*The Economic Review*)

4 'I wanted to ask you something,' he said.
   '*Did you*? What was it?' she said.
   'I don't want you to make fun of me,' he said.
   '*Don't you*?' she replied, enigmatic.
   (D. H. Lawrence: *The Princess and Other Stories*)

5 The composer Stravinsky was asked by Balanchine, the impresario, to choreograph a polka. What Balanchine had not told him was that the music had been commissioned by a circus.
   'Who exactly will be dancing this polka?' asked Stravinsky.
   'Elephants,' came the reply.
   'I see,' said the composer. '*How old*?'
   '*Young*,' said Balanchine.
   'If they're very young,' said Stravinsky, '*I'll do it.*' Well, *they were*; and *he did* – hence the Circus Polka.
   (*The Listener*)

6 Swellings of molten lava from deep down in the earth's mantle heaved up the land to form these highlands. The crust groaned under the tremendous pressure. In the end, the strain was just too much; the crust had to crack, *and it did*.
   (Richard Leakey and Roger Lewin: *People of the Lake*)

TASK SHEET B

Working with a partner, suggest translations for the expressions in italics. Offer alternatives if possible.

1 He has written out, in good readable English prose, exactly what he thinks the original means. His translation deserves to be widely read, *and will be*.
(review of a translation of *The Iliad*, in *The Linguist*)

2 Anyone who wanted to get to know Orwell had *to do so* on his terms and none other.
('Orwell Remembered', in *The Listener*)

3 **Alison** Everything seems very different here now – with you here.
   Helena *Does it?*
   Alison Yes. I was on my own before.
   Helena Now you've got me. So you're not sorry you asked me to stay?
   Alison *Of course not.*
   (John Osborne: *Look Back in Anger*)

4 The alcoholic may drink for no apparent reason. Whether or not the person is aware of why he drinks is questionable; reasons *for so doing* may or may not be conscious.
(F. L. Marcuse: *Hypnosis: Fact and Fiction*)

5 If you want marvellous descriptions by an interesting man of interesting places, and a sense of religion, then this is the book for you. *If not, not.*
(book review, *The Listener*)

6 (The author is stuck in a remote hotel in E. Africa.) I am not by nature a restless or volatile person, forever demanding diversion, yet I do not think I was ever so desperate in my life: *no books, no radio, no argument, no pictures, no news*. I have a temperament ill-adjusted to contemplation. Nobody turned up. Until, on the fourth day, *somebody did*.
(James Cameron: *Point of Departure*)

3 Time: tense, mood, and aspect

Introduction

This section concentrates on the verb – on state and action, being and doing, and on various ways of marking time.

Although each of the four main activities is concerned with a specific aspect of the language (participle forms, passive forms, conditionals, and tenses), there is a close connection between them. A single short passage may contain passives, -*ing* forms, *if*-clauses, all together – not to mention tenses and time markers. This is well illustrated in a passage by Desmond Morris on intention movements:

> . . . he leans forward, as if about to push himself upward. This is the first act he would perform if he were rising. If he were not hesitating, it would only last a fraction of a second . . . Instead, he holds his 'readiness-to-rise' posture, and keeps on holding it.

It is because these four elements are so closely interrelated, and because they are better studied in context than in isolation, that I have used longer passages in this section.

Source language influence

In all four activities, source language influence is an important concern. What we are dealing with here is structure, more than lexis. That is, with the overall way in which a sentence is shaped, rather than with the individual choice of words. This 'shape' is, of course, determined by the structures available to English. Similar structures (-*ing* forms, or the passive) may exist in other languages but they will not necessarily be used as frequently, or in the same way. However, because the thought is set out in English, students will naturally be tempted to reproduce the English structure rather than look for a (possibly) more appropriate structure in their own language. Take for example the use of the passive in activity 3.2, task sheet B, number 2:

> Society of Authors: *You are invited* to the Society's AGM, which *will be followed* by an 'Any Questions' discussion.

This is a characteristic formula in English. Would the same formula be characteristic in the L1? Would it be more usual to word such an invitation in some other way, 'The Society *invites* you to attend the

AGM, after which *there will be* a discussion', or 'We are inviting members to attend the AGM and (to) *take part in* the discussion (which is) *to follow*'? This is not to say that a different formulation <u>must</u> be found, but simply that the English structure should not automatically be imitated.

Target language openings

In speaking of source language influence one may forget that there is a reverse side to the coin. This I would call 'target language openings', by which I mean making use of the potential of the L1 to gain clarity or precision. Consider, for instance, the last sentence of the earlier-quoted example:

He holds his *'readiness-to-rise'* posture, and *keeps on holding it*.

In many languages (Slav languages, for example) the words *keeps on holding* (it) might be expressed through a single verb (*zadržava*). It is possible, too, that in other languages the *'readiness-to-rise'* posture might be expressed with similar economy.

These target language openings or opportunities can easily be missed. This is why I have placed so much stress on oral translation and on comparison of notes based on the oral translation. Often, the best solutions occur when we translate off-the-cuff. Not without thinking, but without too much pondering. And, though it is not always true that 'two heads are better than one', in translation activities it certainly does help to sharpen one's own mind on the grindstone of another.

3.1 The *–ing*, *–ed*, and *–en* forms

PREPARATION

1 Select passages containing *–ing* forms, and participles with *–ed* and *–en* endings.

2 Make up enough task sheets for the whole class. If the students wish to work on longer texts, choose and make up copies of texts like the one in task sheet C (for advanced students).

IN CLASS

1 As a warm-up, you could use some of the material from activity 3.2, for example:

– *Parking prohibited*
– *Cycling on the footpath is not allowed*

Write up ten or twelve notices of this kind on the blackboard and ask the class as a whole to suggest translations.

2 Hand out the task sheets and get the students to work in pairs, translating orally, but noting down their rendering of the phrases in italics.

3 Each pair then discusses their translations with other pairs.

4 Next, discuss with the whole class the most problematic examples in each task sheet, and also those for which two equally valid translations are possible.

COMMENTS

1 In many cases the *–ing* forms will be translated simply by an infinitive (*Seeing is believing / Voir, c'est croire / Videti znači verovati*). But a straightforward equivalent may not always be possible, for example: *You never catch him acting* might be rendered as *On ne le surprend jamais à jouer la comédie*.

2 *–ing* forms frequently occur at the beginning of sentences. In the discussion (*In class*, step 4), one of the questions to consider is how much the word order of the translation has been influenced by the English. (See also activity 2.2.)

TASK SHEET A

With your partner, translate orally the passages below, but note down all suggested translations for the words in italics.

1 *Living in a small hotel* on the left bank in Paris, *moving between contacts* in the working-class suburbs and among students in the Latin Quarter, Tito gained many left-wing international contacts.
(Phyllis Auty: *Tito: A Biography*)

2 '*When translating*, I usually *start by dictating* a quick, rough translation of the foreign language text straight onto a cassette, *bypassing any difficulties*, if necessary *devising ad hoc ways of overcoming them* temporarily, and *striving to get the general hang of the original*, while *allowing the natural rhythm* of the spoken word to give the translation a shape and a flow which will not be lost *by being revised* and polished later on.'
(interview with translator Frederick Fuller)

3 (As a young man, the author had sent a letter to *The Times*.) To my great astonishment, *The Times* published my letter in full. *Looking back on it now*, over the sixteen years which have seen so much worse, it seems to me to have been pretentious.
(James Cameron: *Point of Departure*)

4 A freelancer's life is in a lot of ways freer that other people's, but it demands a great deal of self-discipline. When you are first setting up, a lot of your time will be spent *writing letters of application and CVs, preparing for interviews, hounding your friends for contacts*, and *organizing your time* in a manageable way.
(*The Freelancer*)

5 'Hassan! Look at those flies!', and he pointed to the horrible mass that hung from the ceiling. 'Why have I called you?'
'To drive them away elsewhere,' said Hassan.
'*Driven elsewhere* they always return.'
(E. M. Forster: *A Passage to India*)

TASK SHEET B With your partner, translate orally the passages below, but note down all suggested translations for the words in italics.

1 *Taken prisoner of war*, he (Tito) was transported to a hospital in an old monastery deep in the Russian interior at Sviashk.
(Phyllis Auty: *Tito: A Biography*)

2 The list of rules (in the lodging-house) forbade *cooking in one's room*, or *taking food that did not need cooking to one's room*. No visitors were allowed in one's room at any time for any reason. *Breathing was allowed* as long as it made no noise. The same applied to sleep. Anyone who snored would wake up in the street.
(Clive James: *Unreliable Memoirs*)

3 Trevor Howard was one of the great stage and screen stars of his generation – an actor of enormous power and character of whom Robert Mitchum once said: 'The nice thing about Trevor is that *you never catch him acting.*' It was a compliment he well deserved, since nothing would ever induce him to give a fake performance.
(obituary of Trevor Howard, in *The Guardian*)

4 *Going backward over the day*, I find things of which I am quite certain, other things of which I am almost certain, and other things of which I can become certain by thought.
(Bertrand Russell: *The Problems of Philosophy*)

5 Because there is a certain tension *involved in eating in public*, restaurants employ two major trends to exploit the mood of their diners. The expensive restaurant, to justify high prices, has to overcome the tensions. It does this *by shielding, screening, and partitioning* and also *by keeping lights dim and sounds muffled,* and *by having more staff* than usual so as to reduce waiter-speeds.
(Desmond Morris: *Manwatching*)

6 **Remedies**
In desperation a householder went out at midnight just before Christmas to try to poison the moles in his lawn. To illuminate the mole hills, he turned on the lights of his Jaguar, but the car shot into reverse, *causing £6,000* worth of damage to his house. To make matters worse, an electric heater overturned, *igniting the petrol* and *resulting in his car becoming a write-off*. He finally solved his mole problem with a ton of ready-mixed concrete.
(*The Guardian*)

TASK SHEET C   Translate the passage below from the beginning of line seven.
Concentrate in particular on ways of rendering the expressions with
not, such as *not drinking, not spitting, not speaking your mind*, etc.

This admirable work by Norbert Elias was first published in
German in 1939, and has only now been translated into English
(but, so far as I can judge, most excellently translated). What it
offers is, really, no less that a complete and rounded theory of
civilisation, the origins of 'civilisation', its antecedents, and its later
career.
The sentence which best summarises Elias's theory is as follows:
'*Courtoisie, civilité,* and *civilisation* mark the three stages of social
development. They indicate which society is speaking and being
addressed at a given time.' In the case of *courtoisie,* it is feudal
society speaking, that is to say, the court circles surrounding the
great feudal lords. The word asserts the existence of good manners,
which are 'how people behave at court', as opposed to the bad and
coarse manners of peasants. There are many medieval textbooks of
courtesy, 'table-disciplines' and compendiums for young
noblemen, and their precepts centre upon table-manners – not
drinking direct from the dish, not spitting across the table, not
blowing your nose with the same hand as you use to hold the meat,
not cleaning your teeth on the tablecloth, etc.
The succeeding stage or standard was *civilité.* It is the standard of the
absolutist court, consisting of politeness, good form and restrained
behaviour, not speaking your mind or mentioning what must be
hidden, avoiding all vulgar expressions or over-specific terms. This
standard was given embodiment in French classical tragedy, which
'shows courtly people as they would like to be and, at the same
time, as the absolutist prince wants to see them.'
Let us now proceeed to the third and final stage, that of
'civilisation'. The French term *civilisation* is, apparently, first
found in the writings of the elder Mirabeau, and in its original
usage it signified an active process (i.e. 'civilising', or making
civilised) rather than a condition. It was the rallying cry of the
Physiocrats and of the opposition generally, and it conveyed the
sense that *civilité (ancien régime* politeness and all that) was no
longer enough. *Civilité* represented a false civilisation, against
which should be asserted a 'true' one – 'the civilising of the state,
the constitution, education, and therefore of broader sections of the
population, the liberation from all that was still barbaric or
irrational in existing conditions.'
(P. N. Furbank in *The Listener*)

3.2 Passive forms

1 Make a selection of medium-length passages (eight to fifteen lines) illustrating common uses of passive constructions in English. These should include impersonal constructions with *it*, such as: *It may be seen that/has been observed that/may be concluded that . . .*, etc.

2 Prepare enough copies so that each student has two task sheets.

3 Task sheet C is an example of the kind of extended text you could prepare if you feel the students need further work.

1 As a warm-up, present the class with some typical examples of uses of the passive in English. For instance:

– An opportunity *not to be missed!*
– Applications *must be submitted* by 21 February at the latest.
– Letters to the editor *are welcomed,* but *not all can be acknowledged.*
– The President *is alleged* to be 'indisposed'. His whereabouts, however, *are not known.*
– Rain, possibly turning to sleet or snow, *is expected* in the late afternoon.
– When using this product, *care must be taken* to avoid all contact with the skin.
– These findings have yet *to be confirmed*.

The students should identify the context as precisely as possible, and offer suitable translations. After discussion, invite them to add examples of their own.

2 As a written exercise for work out of class, give each student both task sheets. At home, they should decide which set they prefer to translate, and produce a written translation of each passage in the task sheet.

3 For oral work in class, ask the students to pair up (or 'team up') with others who have translated the same set. (If groups are larger than four, they should be divided.) They then discuss difficulties and compare translations.

1 Although in some examples exact formula-equivalents will exist (in L1) for the English passive forms, most of the passages require extended thought. This is why the activity should first be done in writing.

In step 3, after the discussion, ask the students to discuss the other set, that is, the one they chose not to translate, with anyone who did translate it. This will help to make clear whether there were any special difficulties (ignorance of the subject, lack of interest, or language problems) which influenced the students' choices.

2 Passive forms and passive constructions are so much part of English that they will occur naturally in all kinds of language from the highly technical to the colloquial. Any selection of examples will inevitably be wanting in some respect. (The selection given below, for instance, includes no literary extracts.) However, I have tried to give a reasonably extensive cross-section of the contexts in which passive forms are likely to occur.

3 To end on a more personal note: When I first started looking for examples for this section, I had no trouble in finding model sentences. But when I put them down, torn out of context, I found that they looked depressingly like the archetypal examples from language textbooks: *Translate into the active/passive:*

– *Cain was slain* by Abel

– I *saw* a vessel approaching

Which yields: 'Abel *slew* Cain' and 'A vessel *was seen* approaching (by me)'. But what this does not yield is: Why was the passive (or active) used? Where and how? This is why I have preferred longer texts, ones with a bit of 'elbow-room', because the passive is not just a form or a construction, it is part of a larger context. And to appreciate why it is used, we need also to know what else has been said.

4 This activity might also be done in reverse, by asking students to suggest English translations for signs, notices, etc. common to their own culture.

Although this book is primarily concerned with translation from English, many teachers will – I am sure – be involved with translation into English. This material could serve as a useful starting point for discussion on how to translate brochures and publicity material for international conferences and festivals.

TASK SHEET A

Out of class, translate in writing the passages below. Later, in class, compare your translations with others who have worked on the same texts.

1 In the past *it was thought*, and to a certain extent *still is*, that only those who are emotionally unstable *could be hypnotized*. *It was also believed* that these people when they regained their emotional stability *would no longer be hypnotizable*. Such observations *were based* on only a few cases and failed to realize that when a patient was sick he tended to be dependent.
(F. L. Marcuse: *Hypnosis: Fact and Fiction*)

2 **Guest Houses**

The choice of this type of accommodation is very wide – more than 200 towns and villages offer guest house accommodation. The rooms *are simply furnished* with *shared bathroom*, but may have their own private W.C. Generally speaking, you will find the rooms clean and comfortable, and while *bed linen is provided*, *you are advised* to take your own towels.
(PanAdriatic travel brochure)

3 Whichever party is in power, houses *will have to be built, bought, heated, and lit*; people *will have to be clothed, fed, doctored, and buried*; children *will have to be reared and educated*; taxes *will have to be paid*; food *will have to be grown and processed*. The party approaches to these basic aspects of being alive can only be minimally different.
(Kenneth Hudson: *The Language of Modern Politics*)

4 **Canning of fruit and vegetables: fruit lacquered cans**

These special cans have a layer of golden-coloured lacquer over the inside surface, which prevents the fruit from coming into contact with the tin itself. They *may be used* for all fruits, and are ESSENTIAL for purple or red-coloured fruits, such as blackcurrants and raspberries. Before use, the lacquer *should be examined* to make sure there are no scratches on its surface. Store empty cans upside down in a dry place to prevent rusting and away from strong smells, such as soap and onions, which *may be picked up* by the lacquer and subsequently taint the fruit. Cans *should be rinsed* in clean water before use, and any dents in the rim *should be removed* if good results *are to be secured*. *After the cans have been rinsed,* they *should be inverted to drain*, but *should not be dried* with a cloth as this might scratch the lacquer.
(Marguerite Patten: *500 Recipes: Jams, Pickles, Chutneys*)

TASK SHEET B   Out of class, translate in writing the passages below. Later, in class, compare your translations with others who have worked on the same texts.

1 *It is commonly believed* that women are more emotional than men, and also that they tend to be more timid and less physically aggressive. Although much opposing evidence *may be quoted, none is at all firmly based*, and *it can at least be pointed out* that in most species it is the male who is more aggressive.
(H. J. Eysenck: *Sense and Nonsense in Psychology*)

2 The Society of Authors: *You are invited* to the Society's AGM, which *will be followed by* an 'Any Questions' discussion. Please complete and return the slip below. In order to save costs, *applications will NOT be acknowledged*.
(The Society of Authors newsletter)

3 **Contributions to *The Linguist***
PLEASE READ THE FOLLOWING DIRECTIONS CAREFULLY.
Submitting your manuscript *in the way described* will save the time and expense of unnecessary correspondence. It is essential that papers *be submitted* in their final form, because the printers *will be justified* in charging heavily for rearranging text to accommodate 'second thoughts'. Typographical errors *can be corrected* on the proof, but changes and additions *can only be made* at the author's expense.
(*The Linguist*)

4 **Conditions of contract**
Carrier's name *may be abbreviated* in the ticket, the full name and its abbreviation *being set forth* in carrier's tariffs, conditions of carriage, regulations or timetables; the *agreed stopping places* are those places *set forth* in this ticket or *as shown* in carrier's timetables as *scheduled stopping places* on the passenger's route; carriage *to be performed hereunder* by several successive carriers *is regarded as* a single operation.

Checked baggage will be delivered to bearer of the baggage check. In case of damage to baggage moving in international transportation, complaint *must be made* in writing to carrier forthwith after discovery of damage. In case of delay, complaint *must be made* within 21 days from *date the baggage was delivered*.

Times shown in timetables or elsewhere *are not guaranteed* and form no part of this contract. Schedules *are subject to change* without notice.
(IATA, from the 'small print' on an airline ticket)

TASK SHEET C

In the text below, passive constructions dominate. Before translating, read through the passage, underlining all uses of the passive, such as: 'a traffic road at this point *should be avoided*', 'new residential areas *should be brought back into the city*', 'any development . . . *should be held in check*'.

When translating, think first of the meaning. Then decide what wording would be most suitable. Try not to be too influenced by the (English) use of the passive.

PROPOSALS FOR RESTRUCTURING

KUWAIT

Four architectural firms of international standing (from England, Italy, France, and Finland) were invited by the Government of Kuwait to submit proposals for the reconstruction of a city which had largely disappeared with the oil boom. The general proposals, which covered the city as a whole, were followed by detailed proposals in the form of demonstration buildings. In the first part of this article, we shall be dealing briefly with the four general proposals.

The main task of the four groups of architects was to try to establish principles which might guide the development of the future city. These principles were in essence architectural. They were concerned with the kind of city that might be built for this changing culture and this particular climate. The architects were entirely free to develop their own individual ideas but for the purpose of comparison all proposals were drawn to the same scale and statistics were presented on a comparable basis.

Each scheme had special characteristics and made differing assumptions about the intensity of development within the city, but the four also showed some common points of agreement:

1 All four architects stressed the value of the waterfront as a recreational area for the city and thought that a traffic road at this point should be avoided.

2 All architects agreed that the area immediately surrounding the Sief Palace and harbour should be developed as a special area and that the palace and any government buildings closely associated with it should be designed as a whole.

3 All architects agreed that new residential areas should be brought back into the city. The advantages of bringing people back into the city to increase liveliness and to avoid commuting were stressed.

4 All architects agreed that the 'souk' or bazaar area of the city should be preserved and encouraged in growth. Methods were suggested of linking this to surrounding open areas with shade-creating structures.

5 All submissions regarded the existing green belt as an important recreational space and all considered that any development beyond the fourth ring road should be held in check.

On the basis of this work boundaries could be defined for four action area studies by the architects. The agreement reached was that in each of these action areas one of the groups should be appointed to work out specific planning proposals that could be carried through into building.

(*The Architectural Review*)

<u>VARIATION</u>	**Signs, notices, and instructions**

<u>PREPARATION</u>

1 Collect single sentences taken from public signs, notices, instructions, etc. Each should contain some form of the passive:

– This container *must be kept upright*.
– We regret *NO CREDIT GIVEN*.
– Trespassers *will be prosecuted*.

2 Make up four sets of task sheets (A, B, C, and D) and provide enough copies of each for one quarter of the class.

<u>IN CLASS</u>

1 As a stimulus to discussion, write up on the blackboard a few of the passive forms which often occur in notices, such as:

– *must (not) be / should always be / is to be* . . .
– *not allowed / prohibited / not permitted*
– *You are reminded / informed / requested / expected* . . .

2 Ask the class to call out any public signs containing these or similar words (in English). They should also say where they would expect to see the words (inside a church, at the entrance to a park, on a cardboard box, etc.). For each example, they should suggest an equivalent in their own language – not necessarily a translation, but the wording they would expect in the same context.

3 Divide the class into four groups, A, B, C, and D, and give each student in each group the corresponding task sheet. Each group should then divide into pairs to discuss their set of examples.

Once again, they should find a likely context for each and suggest an L1 equivalent. When ready, they compare notes with others who have worked on the same set.

4 For further work, tell the students to imagine that their town has been selected for an important international congress or sports championship. Signs and notices in English will be needed at certain key places in the town (for example, at the railway station, on the main square, in hotel reception areas, etc.). Each student should make his or her own list of suggested notices, with the place in which they would appear, and also indicate any prominent signs or notices in the L1 which would need to be translated into English.

<u>COMMENTS</u>

1 The language of signs and notices is, in a sense, a special language with its own set forms and expressions. The same message in one language may be expressed in quite different words in another: *No Parking / Défense de stationner, No cameras allowed / Il est interdit de prendre des photos, Danger de mort / Lebensgefahr / Chi tocca muore!* This is why, in this activity, the importance of context is stressed, to remind students that they should interpret the message in terms of their own culture – which is not necessarily the same as translating the words.

2 See also activities 1.1 and 5.2.

TASK SHEET A

Passive forms are very common in all kinds of materials designed for public information (signs, notices, regulations, etc.). Below are some of those most often seen. With a partner, look at the items in your task sheet and decide where you would be most likely to see each one (in a hotel, on a building site, on a public notice-board, etc.). Decide in each case what would be the usual wording for a similar sign or notice in your own culture. If a direct translation would be out of place, suggest a suitable equivalent.

1 Guests *are courteously reminded* that *no visitors are permitted* in the rooms after 10 p.m.

2 The mixture *to be taken* three times daily after meals.

3 We regret that no change *can be given* for the telephone.

4 We apologize for the interruption. Normal transmission *will be resumed* as soon as possible.

5 Light showers *may be expected* in the early afternoon. In the north-east, these may develop into thunderstorms, possibly *accompanied by* hail.

6 Prams and pushcarts *must be folded and carried* on the escalator.

7 Please note that latecomers *will NOT be admitted* until the first interval.

8 Notice: Bathing and fishing *strictly prohibited*.

TASK SHEET B   Passive forms are very common in all kinds of materials designed for public information (signs, notices, regulations, etc.). Below are some of those most often seen. With a partner, look at the items in your task sheet and decide where you would be most likely to see each one (in a hotel, on a building site, on a public notice-board, etc.). Decide in each case what would be the usual wording for a similar sign or notice in your own culture. If a direct translation would be out of place, suggest a suitable equivalent.

1 Sorry – *NO CREDIT given!*

2 *Right of admission reserved.*

3 All payment by cheque *must be accompanied* by a valid banker's card.

4 All complaints *should be addressed in writing* to the manager.

5 TRESPASSERS *WILL BE PROSECUTED.*

6 NO PARKING AT ANY TIME – *Your car may be removed.*

7 If you have any complaint concerning this product *it should be returned*, together with your receipt, to the manufacturer.

8 Please check your change, as *mistakes cannot later be rectified.*

TASK SHEET C   Passive forms are very common in all kinds of materials designed for public information (signs, notices, regulations, etc.). Below are some of those most often seen. With a partner, look at the items in your task sheet and decide where you would be most likely to see each one (in a hotel, on a building site, on a public notice-board, etc.). Decide in each case what would be the usual wording for a similar sign or notice in your own culture. If a direct translation would be out of place, suggest a suitable equivalent.

1 *Right of way restricted* to tenants and visitors only.

2 These doors *must be kept clear* at all times.

3 Rooms *are to be vacated* by midday at the latest.

4 These premises *are protected* by guard-dogs.

5 Applications *must be completed* in four copies. Each copy *must be signed and returned*, together with four passport-size photographs, to the following address.

6 For official use only. Nothing *to be written* in the space below.

7 Note: Airport tax *is not included* in the price of the fare, and *must be paid* locally on arrival or departure.

8 The management *cannot be held responsible* for the theft or loss of valuables *not deposited* for safekeeping at the reception.

TASK SHEET D

Passive forms are very common in all kinds of materials designed for public information (signs, notices, regulations, etc.). Below are some of those most often seen. With a partner, look at the items in your task sheet and decide where you would be most likely to see each one (in a hotel, on a building site, on a public notice-board, etc.). Decide in each case what would be the usual wording for a similar sign or notice in your own culture. If a direct translation would be out of place, suggest a suitable equivalent.

1 *Entry restricted* to vehicles not exceeding ten tons.

2 HELMETS *MUST BE WORN* ON SITE

3 This is a place of worship. Silence *is requested* during services.

4 This garment *should NOT be washed* by machine.

5 We regret that goods *cannot be exchanged* after purchase.

6 All passes *must be shown* at the door.

7 No applications *can be accepted* after the closing date.

8 Please note: a service charge *will be automatically added* to your bill. This *is done* in order to discourage the practice of tipping. Staff have strict instructions that no gratuities or other forms of remuneration *are to be accepted*.

3.3 Conditionals

PREPARATION

1 Choose passages that illustrate various types of conditional sentences, such as:

– *If I were* doing the part, *I would be* very calm.
– *If any unity is to be ascribed* to the Victorian era in England, it must be found in two governing conditions.

2 Make up two sets of task sheets like task sheets A and B, and provide copies of both for each student in the class.

3 Examples of longer texts for further work are given in task sheets C and D. The material in the task sheets is intended primarily for written work to be done out of class. Give the students copies of task sheets A and B and ask them to translate any two items from each.

IN CLASS

1 When the students have returned their translations, present a selection of the different translations offered for certain key phrases. These should be discussed by the class as a whole.

2 Follow up the discussion with a short oral activity based on the translation of lines from songs and poems. For instance:

– *If you were* the only girl in the world, and *I was* the only boy . . . (popular song)

– *If you knew* Susie like I know Susie, oh, oh, oh what a gal!
(popular song)
– Was he free? Was he happy? The question is absurd: Had
anything been wrong, *we should certainly have heard*.
(W. H. Auden, from 'The Unknown Citizen')

COMMENTS

1 In the material, I have been able to offer only a small range of
examples. I have tried, however, to make the sample representative
by including passages from both written and spoken language, and
by including a variety of styles and registers.

The main aim here is not to 'teach' the students more about the
conditional, but to get them to reflect on the similarities and the
differences in usage between their own language and English. Is the
conditional form always needed? Could it be replaced by, say, a
simple present or future tense?

2 If you are looking for further examples for the oral activity, you
will find a useful starting-point in the Index of First Lines of poetry
anthologies (under *If, Were, Had*, etc.). And no doubt the students
will be able to add examples of their own from songs.

TASK SHEET A

Translate two of the passages below, paying special attention to the
phrases in italics.

1 So far as I know ours is the only language in which it has been
found necessary to give a name to the piece of prose which is
described as 'the purple patch'; *it would not have been necessary to
do so unless it were characteristic.*
(Somerset Maugham: *A Writer's Notebook*)

2 (The writer is discussing the plan for a new housing scheme.)
Supposing that it could actually be put into operation, the advantages
of the plan are obvious. Living around a green belt *would almost
certainly promote sociability*, and it is an important detail that each
of the Community Centres *would only be serving* about 1,000
people, all of whom *might be expected* to know one another by
sight. The green spaces, the absence of smoke, and the ever-
running hot water *would make for* health and cleanliness, and the
children *would grow up* in the constant society of others of the
same age.
(George Orwell, review of the Reilly Plan)

3 The local KOMPAS office will allocate the reserved apartment
upon your arrival at your resort. Since KOMPAS local offices
work within fixed hours, *we would not advise you* to book this type
of accommodation *if your arrival in the resort* is later than 20.00
hours.
(PanAdriatic tourist brochure)

IF YOU KNEW SOMEONE WITH CANCER WOULD YOU HELP? THIS IS KATHLEEN GILLETT. SHE HAS CANCER.

NOW YOU KNOW HER.

It's all too easy to imagine that cancer only ever happens to other people.

That it will never affect you or your family.

And perhaps you'll be lucky. But what about the many thousands of people like Kathleen Gillett, who are not so fortunate?

You don't know them. But you can make all the difference to their lives by giving your support to Cancer Relief.

Our Macmillan nurses are trained to care for both the physical and the mental pain this ruthless disease causes patients and their families.

It's their skill, and that of the local GP and district nurse, that allows patients to remain at home rather than in hospital.

And their care that allows life to go on as normally and with as much dignity as this cruel disease will allow.

But it's your generosity that buys this care. That helps to make a life for those who live with cancer.

Please send your contributions to Major H. C. L. Garnett CBE, Room xxxx, Cancer Relief Macmillan fund, 15/19 Britten Street, London SW3 3TZ. Tel: 01-351 7811.

Cancer Relief HELP TO BEAR THE COST OF CARE
Macmillan fund Registered as the National Society for Cancer Relief Regd. No. 261017

TASK SHEET B

Translate two of the passages below, paying special attention to the phrases in italics.

1 *If any real unity is to be ascribed* to the Victorian era in England, *it must be found* in two governing conditions: first, there was no great war, and secondly, the whole period was marked by interest in religious questions.
(G. M. Trevelyan: *Illustrated English Social History*)

2 *If an observer is asked to judge* the size of an object at a considerable distance away from him, his judgement will not normally conform to the size of the image projected on his retina, but to *the size of the object he would see if it were at the distance* at which such an object is usually viewed. Indeed, he may be able to estimate the 'real' sizes of objects when they are quite a long distance away.
(M. D. Vernon: *The Psychology of Perception*)

3 (The passage below is from an interview with the actor Alec McCowen, here reminiscing about his work with Alfred Hitchcock.)

Hitchcock was supposed to be terrible to actors, but he was the most loving man towards me. He left a film very much to its own devices, although he was very strict about reaction shots. The only lengthy advice he gave me was when I was supposed to arrest the 'necktie' murderer. Of course, I came on like Kirk Douglas. But Hitchock said: *'If I were doing the part* – and of course I'm not, so it's up to you – but *if I were doing it, I would be very calm, I might lean against the wall, I might sigh*, and *I would say very quietly*: "You're not wearing your necktie." But it's up to you.' So of course I did exactly as he suggested.
(*The Times*)

4 (The author is speaking of the function of language in politics.)
The use of slogans as a method of influencing people is not necessarily unreasonable. A skilful leader of men, *however complicated were* his own thought processes, *would need to express* his doctrines in predigested form *for them to be* widely accepted, and, for the purpose of mass action, this *could most conveniently be done* by inventing slogans.
(Robert Thouless: *Straight and Crooked Thinking*)

TASK SHEET C   In translating the passage below, pay particular attention to the phrases in italics. When you have read the text, and before you translate it, look at the notes that follow it.

INTENTION MOVEMENTS
(Get-ready actions that signal future intentions)

When we are *about to take action*, we often make small, preparatory movements. These can act as clues, revealing what we intend to do, and they are called Intention Movements. *If we were prepared to* plunge straight into the new activity, *whatever it might happen to*
5 *be, we would not hesitate*, and the 'starting' movements *would grow smoothly* into the full pattern of behaviour. But, *if for some reason we are hesitant*, then the first small piece of the action is all that we do. We start, then stop; start, then stop again. So there is a double clue: *something is making us want to act*, but *something else is*
10 *stopping us*.

In social situations, the classic Intention Movement is the 'chair-grasp'. Host and guest *have been talking for some time*, but now the host has an appointment to keep and must get away. His urge to go is held in check by his desire not to be rude to his guest. *If he did not*
15 *care about his guest's feelings, he would simply get up* out of his chair and announce his departure. This is what his body wants to do, but his politeness glues his body to the chair and refuses to let him rise. It is at this point that he performs the chair-grasp Intention Movement. He continues to talk to the guest and listen to him, but
20 *he leans forward* and graps the arms of the chair *as if about to push himself upward*. This is the first act *he would perform if he were rising. If he were not hesitating, it would only last* a fraction of a second. *He would* lean, push, rise, and be up. But now, instead, it lasts much longer. He holds his 'readiness-to-rise' posture and *keeps*
25 *on holding it*. It is *as if his body has frozen* at the get-ready moment.

Starting from repose.

The host, in performing this extended Intention Movement, *may be making a deliberate gesture*, hoping that the guest will take the hint, or he may be unaware that he is doing it. A sensitive guest will, however usually respond fairly quickly. He, too, *may do this*
30 *unconsciously*, or *he may read* the sign clearly and become fully aware that he has outstayed his welcome.

When we wish to rise, we adopt the Intention Movement of getting up from the chair, and this posture often acts as a clue that we want to terminate an encounter. (After Siddons, 1822).

(Desmond Morris: *Manwatching*)

Notes

Below are some brief notes on points of language which should be considered when translating the text.

Line 3 *If we were prepared* . . . Compare this with (*Line 6*) *But if . . . we are hesitant* . . . Why the change of structure? Could the present simple also be used in the first sentence?

Line 5 *would grow smoothly into the full pattern of behaviour* . . . Is the meaning clear? If not, actually make such a movement and think how it would continue. Should *grow* be translated by a different verb, such as *turn, develop, continue?*

Line 7 . . . *the first small piece of the action* . . . Why *the* action? Can *first small piece* be translated literally?

Line 7 *is all that we do* . . . Could these words come earlier, for example, after *then* (*Line 7*)?

Line 11 *Host and guest.* Why not *the* host, *the* guest? . . . *have been talking for some time.* Note the tense.

Line 14 . . . *not to be rude to his guest.* Can this be translated by a synonym like *not to offend?*

Line 17 *his politeness glues his body to the chair and refuses to let him rise.* This sounds rather odd in English. Consider alternative wordings in translation, such as the use of passive forms: *his body is glued to the chair.*

Line 22 *If he were not hesitating* . . . Note the tense.

Line 23 *He would . . . rise and be up.* What translations are possible for *be up?*

Line 23 *now . . . it lasts much longer.* Should *it* be replaced by a noun in translation, for example (his/the) *action?*

Line 27 *hoping that the guest will take the hint.* Note and comment on the various ways other students translate *take the hint.*

Line 30 *He . . . may do this unconsciously.* How is *this* translated?

Line 31 *he has outstayed his welcome.* There is a difference between *stayed too long* and *outstayed his welcome.* Does this come through in the translation?

TASK SHEET D

In translating the text below, pay particular attention to the *if-clauses*.

The trouble with tea is that originally it was quite a good drink. So a group of the most eminent British scientists put their heads together, and made complicated biological experiments to find a way of spoiling it . . .

There are some occasions when you must not refuse a cup of tea, otherwise you are judged an exotic and barbarous bird without any hope of ever being able to take your place in civilised society.

If you are invited to an English home, at five o'clock in the morning you get a cup of tea . . . Then you have tea for breakfast; then you have tea at eleven o'clock in the morning; then after lunch; then you have tea for tea; then after supper; and again at eleven o'clock at night.

You must not refuse any additional cups of tea under the following circumstances: if it is hot; if it is cold; if you are tired; if anybody thinks that you might be tired; if you are nervous; if you are gay; before you go out; if you are out; if you have just returned home; if you feel like it; if you do not feel like it; if you have had no tea for some time; if you have just had a cup.

(George Mikes: *How to be an Alien*)

3.4 Time: tenses, adverbs, and prepositions

PREPARATION

1 Select passages which cover a range of tenses in English, and which also include time markers such as *until, by, previously, then, now, ago, after, since,* etc.

2 Prepare three task sheets, A, B, and C, and make enough copies of each for one third of the class.

3 The task sheets should preferably be given to the students in advance, to be translated in writing. Discussion in class can then be based on their various written translations. If this is not possible, the activity can be done orally, with only the expressions in italics being written down. The activity is then carried out as follows:

IN CLASS

1 The students work in groups of three. Each student in the group has a copy of the same task sheet. Individually, they note down their translations of all the expressions in italics. (For this step, set a time-limit of about ten minutes.) The students then compare their renderings with those of others in the group, concentrating in particular on points of difference.

2 Ask each group to exchange task sheets with another. In turn, they suggest off-the-cuff oral translations of material in the new task sheets. Members of the listening group can then compare these suggestions with their own written notes. Any unresolved points of contention can later be put to the whole class in group discussion.

COMMENTS

1 The notion of time *past, present,* and *future* is common to all human beings, but the way in which time is perceived and divided up may differ greatly from language to language. To take just one example – the use in English of reported speech:

> We went to Cana of Galilee, where a little girl was offering wine jars for sale. They were the authentic ones used in the miracle. *If they were too big she had* a smaller size indoors; yes, the small ones *were* authentic too.

To the English speaker, it seems quite natural to report past events in the past tense. In other languages, it may be quite natural to report the past (or even the future) in the present tense.

In this activity, then, it is important that the students should not slavishly follow the tense patterns of the English text, but should look for the most appropriate tense in their own language.

2 Task sheet C in activity 3.3 is also highly relevant to this activity.

TASK SHEET A

Translate orally the passages below, but note down your rendering of all words in italics, that is, the expression which you feel best translates these words in context.

1 During the last quarter of the (19th) century large numbers of emigrant farmers *were flowing* into the Great Plains (of the USA). *By 1890, 'the frontier' had disappeared.*
(Winston Churchill: *A History of the English Speaking Peoples*)

2 At informal conversational gatherings, it is common for a wife to look interested when her husband *tells* an anecdote and to feed him with appropriate leads and cues, although in fact she *has heard* the anecdote many times and knows that *the show her husband is making of telling something for the first time* is only a show.
(Erving Goffmann: *The Presentation of Self in Everyday Life*)

3 We went to Cana of Galilee, where a little girl *was offering* wine jars for sale. They *were* the authentic ones used in the miracle. *If they were* too big *she had* a smaller size indoors; yes, the small ones *were* authentic too.
(Evelyn Waugh: *Labels*)

4 **Proposals for Restructuring Kuwait**

The draft prepared for these architectural studies stated:

The Old City of Kuwait *has now largely disappeared.* There are still some traces of its physical form and architectural character in some of the residential areas that remain in the market, but a new

road pattern *has now been established*. Large areas of the Old City *have been cleared* and the new main shops *are being developed* along wide and busy roads. Car traffic *is rapidly increasing* and vacant plots *are being increasingly used* for parking. The character and coherence that the Old City possessed *is vanishing* but development by modern buildings *has not replaced this* by anything *that can yet mark* the new City of Kuwait as a great capital city.
(*The Architectural Review*)

TASK SHEET B

Translate orally the passages below, but note down your rendering of all words in italics, that is, the expression which you feel best translates these words in context.

1 *By 1848* some five thousand miles of railroads *had been built* in the United Kingdom. Coal and iron production *had doubled*. Engineering *was making great, though as yet hesitating, strides*. All the steps *were being taken*, not by Government, but by enterprises throughout the country, which *were to make* Britain the greatest industrial power of the nineteenth-century world.
(Winston Churchill: *A History of the English Speaking Peoples*)

2 *Until he became acquainted* with the operas of Mozart, Haydn *had composed* works for the stage with some regularity. *He had been taking a pride in these* and especially in 'Armida', the last composed for Esterháza, *but once he recognized* the superiority of Mozart's works in this field, without any feeling of jealousy, he lost interest in composing operas.
(Neil Butterworth: *Haydn, His Life and Times*)

3 At the beginning of one rainy season, three and a half million years ago, Sadiman, a volcano due east of Laetoli, *was erupting steadily, showering thin layers of ash* on the surrounding countryside.
(Richard Leakey and Roger Lewin: *People of the Lake*)

4 *Until a car is produced* that's impossible to lock yourself out of.
Until a car is produced that *will never get broken* into.
Until a car is produced that *will never have* a flat battery.
Until a car is produced that *will never run out of* petrol.
Until a car is produced that *will never have a punctured tyre*.
There's a part that *should be fitted* onto every car that's made.

Until a car is produced that's impossible to lock yourself out of.

Until a car is produced that will never have a flat battery.

Until a car is produced that will never run out of petrol.

Until a car is produced that will never have a punctured tyre.

Until then.

There's a part that should be fitted onto every car that's made.

(The 'part that should be fitted' is the RAC badge)

TASK SHEET C

In the text below, certain verbs have been given only in the infinitive form. Choose the tense you consider most suitable, then check your suggestions against the original wording at the end of the text.

For each of the spaces, note the verb form you would use in a translation of the text. (It is not necessary to translate the whole text, unless you wish to do so.) Compare your suggestions with those of others.

Letter from Timbuktu

Strangled by the sands of time

For hundreds of years its very name (1) (*be*)_____ a synonym for the most remote place on earth, but today Timbuktu (2) (*face*)_____ a new kind of extremity. From the 13th century onwards this forbidden city (3) (*carry on*)_____ an impenetrable existence in the heart of Africa. But to its inhabitants and those merchants able to converge on this crossroads of the ancient caravan routes, the town on the fringes of the desert (4) (*be*)_____ a haven from the unyielding harshness of the Sahara, a place of rich grazing for cattle and camels, a university town, a revered centre of worship and a market place of both commercial and cultural exchange.

During the last two decades, however, the desert (5) (*reclaim*)_____ Timbuktu. There (6) (*be*) _____ drought here for the past 15 years; for the past four years it (7) (be) _____ increasingly severe and this year the area (8) (*have*)_____ only half as much rain as in the previous year. The sands (9) (*move*)_____ south. Every year the encroachment (10) (*continue*) _____ .

Now the desert (11) (*sweep*)_____ around the town and (12) (*surround*)_____ it entirely. Occasionally it is possible to glimpse beneath the dust the baked clay surface of what was once a fertile loam. But that is rare. Huge dunes of sand (13) (*creep*)_____ onwards, thousands of tons at the rate of 20 miles a year. The fine white dust (14) (*fall*) _____ imperceptibly from the heavens. There is an apocalyptic quality to living with the earth above your head for so long.

Twenty years ago it (15) (*be*) _____ possible to arrive in Timbuktu by boat along a canal dug from the Niger river. Today, the channel is entirely dry, its side cracked and crumbled, with heaps of old rubbish on its bed. Even the mighty Niger dries up; in a good year it now flows for only seven months.

(*The Times*)

KEY TO TASK

Original wording:

1 has been
2 faces
3 has carried on
4 was
5 has been reclaiming
6 has been
7 has been
8 has had

9 are moving
10 continues
11 has swept
12 surrounded
13 are creeping
14 falls
15 was

4 Concepts and notions

We dissect nature along lines laid down by our native language. Language is not simply a reporting device for experience but a defining framework for it.

(Benjamin Whorf)

Introduction

In his *Life of Johnson*, Boswell recounts a short conversation he had with the Doctor one day after church (see activity 5.7). They were discussing Berkeley's theory that things do not exist in themselves. They exist only in the mind, as collections of ideas. Boswell then remarked that, although we know this is not so, it is impossible to refute the theory. 'I shall never forget,' he says, 'the alacrity with which Johnson answered, striking his foot with mighty force against a large stone, till he rebounded from it, "I refute it *thus*!"'

Johnson was arguing for common sense: the stone is there because it is there! I mention the anecdote because it ties up with that age-old question of language: Do things, ideas, and concepts exist if we do not have words to describe them? Common sense tells us: of course they do. If we do not have in our language a word for, say *pebble, rock*, or *boulder,* we simply speak of a 'small stone' or of a 'big stone'. The pebble is there, lying on the river bed, even if we do not see it as 'a pebble'.

But when we move from things to ideas (concepts and notions), common sense is no longer enough. We cannot kick the stone to prove it is there – because there is no stone. Which is why, perhaps, we speak in English of 'abstract' nouns – *valour, courtesy, concupiscence, evil.* The words themselves do not refer to any concrete, tangible thing.

Thus, for example, when Sir Walter Raleigh laid his cloak in the mud for Queen Elizabeth to walk on, this was an act of courtesy, not courtesy itself. The notion of courtesy can include many different acts.

Though we may find the equivalent of such words in a dictionary, they are rarely identical in meaning.

Before turning to some specific examples of what we shall be dealing with in this section, I should like to say a brief word about the opening quotation.

Dissecting nature

Benjamin Whorf's words 'We dissect nature along lines laid down by our native language' – are so familiar that they have become, in a sense, one of the 'great truths' of language. The formulation is persuasive but it is also, I feel, slightly misleading. 'Dissecting' suggests cutting up into parts or pieces. It also implies that these different pieces in different languages are separate.

If instead of 'dissecting nature' we were to think rather of 'drawing from nature' along lines determined by our native language, this would suggest that we all draw from a common source. And, though we may combine experience in different ways, much of it will be shared.

To take just one example, a concept broad enough to be found in some form in almost any language – that of *information*. What is information? We can point to examples of information (brochures, notices, reports, etc.), but not to information itself. It is not a stone we can kick.

Consider some of the expressions (in English) associated with different kinds of information, or with ways of conveying it: *propaganda, publicity, advertising, broadcasting, teaching, preaching, publishing, proclaiming, diffusing, giving witness, testifying*, etc., and all the associated nouns (*sermon, tract, speech, report*). Equivalents for most of these terms may be found in other languages, but they will rarely cover precisely the same area. The expressions are overlapping circles. *Publicité* in French overlaps with both *advertising* and *publicity* in English. *Diffusion* overlaps with *broadcasting* and even with *publicity drive*. And *propaganda*, which one would expect to have much the same meaning in all languages, has generally negative overtones in English which are not felt in languages which can use propaganda as a synonym for *advertising*. The circles overlap, but rarely match exactly.

And so I suggest that language does not dissect nature, but rather combines experience in different ways.

About the activities

This section is primarily concerned with the ways in which abstract concepts (such as *possibility, causality*, and *perception*) are given concrete expression in language.

The first three activities, headed *Choice of words*, may be seen as an introduction to the following three. Here the focus is on words rather than concepts. What is the precise meaning of a word in a given context? What difference does it make if a slightly different expression is used? For example, if a worker asks for a medical certificate, does the doctor decide he is suffering from *stress and overwork*, or that he is a *malingerer*? If a man has killed, is his crime *murder* or *manslaughter*?

One of the questions that activities 4.1–3 will raise is: what would be the most suitable L1 equivalent for this word or expression? And, by extension, what can be done if the expression does not exist in the L1?

In the remaining three activities, the purpose is essentially the same: to explore the range of expressions that the source language and the L1 commonly associate with a particular concept, and to discover whether there is any real difference between them. For instance, what difference is there between *perceive, notice, see, realize*, and *be aware*? To ask why in one context we might say 'Suddenly *I realized*', in another 'Suddenly *it dawned upon me*'. And, yet again, to find out more precisely where the two languages overlap and where they do not.

4.1 Choice of words: Call my bluff

PREPARATION

1 Look for passages containing unfamiliar words (that is, words you have never seen before) or familiar words used in an unusual sense, for example, *curing*, for drying concrete.

2 Make up two sets of task sheets, A and B, and provide enough copies so that half the class, working in groups of three, has task sheet A, and the other half task sheet B.

3 For each word, make three separate cards by pasting the task sheet onto thin cardboard and cutting between each definition. (This will provide a permanent resource for future use.) One card gives a short definition of the true meaning of the word. The other two give imaginary definitions.

In the examples in the task sheets, all the words are drawn from material to be used in the next activity (4.2).

IN CLASS

1 Divide the students into groups of three. Each group has one set of definitions (task sheet A or B).

For a few minutes, let them discuss which they think the true definition is. When they have made their choice, they call you over. Listen to what they say, then (quietly!) reveal which the true definition is.

2 Explain to the students that they will be working in two teams. Each team has a different set (from task sheet A or B). Team A begins. They present their three definitions to team B – speaking, not reading. Team B then decide which definition they think is true. After a short discussion, they tell team A their decision. Team A listen, and then reveal the answer.

The game is played again using team B's words.

3 (Optional) Give the students fresh sets of definitions, and ask them to work with a different team.

COMMENTS

1 In addition to being an enjoyable language activity in its own right, 'Call my bluff' is also a useful warm-up activity for translation work on texts involving unfamiliar terms. This is why the material here has been chosen from texts the students will later translate.

When the students later meet one of the words (for example, *rubbling*) in a text, it will already be in a sense familiar to them. This familiarity is of help in discussing, for instance:

a. If the word does not appear in the dictionary, what strategy should be used in translation? Retain the English word, *rubbling*? Find a descriptive equivalent – *fouiller dans le débris*? Invent a new word – *ruševanje, fouillardise* . . .?

b. If the word does appear in the dictionary (*narcolepsy, anosmia*), should it be used as a scientific term or would a colloquial expression be more suitable? Does the writer expect the reader to understand the term, or does he/she offer any help? If so, where and why? How much help is given in the text?

2 It is important to stress that this activity is a game, not a test of knowledge. Reassure the students that they are not expected to know the meaning of the words (and if by chance they do, ask them not to give the game away!). Remind them, too, that in the oral presentation they are free to elaborate on the definitions given on the cards. Only the person with the true definition should stay as close as possible to the original wording.

3 'Call my bluff' is based on a BBC television show. For a similar exercise, 'The Devil's Dictionary', see Maley and Duff: *Drama Techniques in Language Learning*.

KEY TO TASKS

Task sheet A
1 b), 2 a), and 3 b) are true; all the others are bluff.

Task sheet B
1 a), 2 c), and 3 a) are true; all the others are bluff.

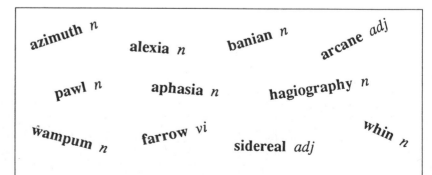

azimuth *n*   alexia *n*   banian *n*   arcane *adj*

pawl *n*   aphasia *n*   hagiography *n*

wampum *n*   farrow *vi*   sidereal *adj*   whin *n*

All these words are in the fourth edition (1989) of the Oxford Advanced Learner's Dictionary.

TASK SHEET A

1a anosmia
A Mediterranean creeper, found mainly in Albania, Corfu, and Western Greece. Noted for its bright vermillion flowers. Related to the family of *bougainvillaea*.

1b anosmia
The loss of the sense of smell. Some people are born with anosmia, in others it develops from a variety of causes and is known as non-congenital anosmia. There is no common word in English (such as blind or deaf) to describe the loss of this sense.

1c anosmia
A word of Greek origin, meaning 'resistance to disease or infection', from the Greek *nosos* = disease. As in: 'The inhabitants of Baluchistan have a high rate of anosmia, owing to the purity of their air, water, and food.'

2a circadian rhythms
These are the rhythms by which animals respond to the changes of light and darkness according to the seasons. They are an internal reflection of the Earth's 24-hour cycle in the animal.

2b circadian rhythms
A term used in music to describe sensuous, irresistible melodies, which linger on in the mind. The reference is to Circe, who was noted in Greek mythology for her powers of enchantment.

2c circadian rhythms
An expression used in computer terminology to account for the difference in speed with which information is provided on a given circuit. Hence the expressions 'high circadian' and 'low circadian'.

3a narcolepsy
A legal term, currently used to cover crimes connected with trafficking in drugs and stimulants, as in : 'The accused was convicted on grounds of narcolepsy, but was cleared of bribery and corruption.'

3b narcolepsy
Is a medical expression for uncontrollable attacks of sleepiness, and was first used in the 1870s. The main symptom is a sudden loss of consciousness during moments of emotional excitement. The condition is related to epilepsy.

3c narcolepsy
A psychiatric term for what is more commonly known as paranoia or persecution complex. It comes from the Gypsy word *nark*, meaning nose. Narcolepsy is fear of authority, i.e. of those who are nosy.

TASK SHEET B

1a gazumping
This is an unfair practice in property dealing. It means raising the price of a house after the final offer has been made. The origin of the word is unknown.

1b gazumping
Means having fun, having a good time, or, as they used to say, carousing. At New Year, there is much gazumping in the streets - and elsewhere.

1c gazumping
Is a colloquial term used in the gas industry to justify price rises. What is said in private is : 'We'll have to do some gazumping.' What is said in public is : 'The cost of gas will, unfortunately, have to be increased.'

2a rubbling
A slang expression, used mainly by journalists, to describe long, boring parts of speeches or interviews. Thus, 'Let's cut the rubbling' means 'Let's edit the speech to leave out the long bits.'

2b rubbling
An old-fashioned word still used by women in some rural communities. It means to beat washing by a stream using heavy flat stones. Hence the saying: 'All stains come out with rubbling - except the stains on your soul.'

2c rubbling
An expression heard mainly in New York and other large American cities. It means the rescuing of decorative sculpture from buildings about to be torn down.

3a curing
In the building trade, this means keeping concrete moist for some time after it has been laid, so that the water it contains can complete the chemical action that takes place as the concrete hardens.

3b curing
This is a ceremony performed in many small parishes in England, when a new priest - or curate - comes to take over from the retiring priest. All the people in the parish contribute a little money for the 'curing', which is a modest tea party held in the church hall.

3c curing
An Asiatic bird of the starling family, having more colourful plumage. It is particularly common in south China, hence its name *avis cantoniensis*. The more common name 'curing' is probably derived from the Chinese 'qu ling'.

4.2 Choice of words: definitions and distinctions

1 You will need two collections of passages, one for *Definitions* (task sheets A and B) the other for *Distinctions* (task sheets C and D). There will, of course, be considerable overlap between the two. But in each there should be a clear emphasis, either on *definition*, that is, where the writer explains a term (familiar or unfamiliar) in his or her own words:

> *Circadian rhythms* are the internal reflection of the Earth's 24-hour cycle in the animal.

or on *distinction*, where the writer draws attention to a difference in meaning between two almost identical expressions:

> *Tiredness and fatigue* are by no means synonymous. We may feel *tired and sleepy without being unduly fatigued.*

2 Prepare a complete set of task sheets A, B, C, and D, and make enough copies of each for the whole class.

3 You should preferably give the students time to think about the material out of class. Each student should have all the material, both *Definitions* and *Distinctions*. The passages do not have to be fully translated, but the rendering of all expressions in italics should be noted down.

In class, in groups of three to five, the students then compare and discuss their ideas.

If there is no time for preparation, the work can be done orally in class, as follows:

1 Give each group one set of task sheets either from *Definitions* or from *Distinctions*. Together, they discuss ways of translating the expressions in italics, and note down the best suggestions.

2 Each group then exchanges notes with others who have worked on the same sets.

3 (Optional) Give the students all the material, for class discussion. Those who have worked on a particular set should raise any problems or unresolved disagreements they have had, and the others in the class offer their own opinions.

1 It must be stressed that this is an exercise in translation, not a test of general knowledge. Whether or not we agree with the writers' definitions or distinctions is relatively unimportant. The task is to translate what is said, not what we think ought to be said. For this reason, I would recommend using dictionaries for this activity.

2 How well a distinction can be made depends partly on the clarity of the writer's thought, and partly on how well the same distinction can be reflected in our own language. If in our own language we have words comparable to those used in the source language, for example *tourist/traveller, touriste/voyageur, turist/putnik*, we are likely to use them and think no further.

But if in our own language we do not have the words, then we do have to think further. Do I understand the distinction? Is there really any difference (say, between *aptitude, ability* and *skill*)? Is the distinction not made in my own language, or is it perhaps not considered necessary?

Even when we do understand the distinction, if we do not have suitable words to express it in our own language we may feel at a loss. A simple and obvious example is that of the words used to describe the divisions of the day.

In English, in addition to *day/night, morning/afternoon*, we also have *dawn, sunrise, early morning, mid-morning, noon, midday, late afternoon, dusk, twilight, evening*, etc. And yet, when it comes to greetings we are effectively restricted to four: *Good morning, Good afternoon, Good evening, Good night*. (*Good-day*, being somewhat old-fashioned, usually has overtones either of rudeness or of servility.) Yet many languages have greetings which allow for finer distinctions. It is almost impossible to translate into English a remark I heard recently from a Hungarian workman who had arrived at nine a.m. to complete a plastering job: '*Jó reggelt kivánnok . . .*' then, correcting himself, '*Vagy esetleg jó napot.*' Both mean, roughly, 'Good morning' in English. But in Hungarian there is a distinction between 'Good-morning-before-breakfast' and 'Good-morning-after-breakfast'!

Much writing – particularly technical, scientific, medical, and legal literature – rests upon fine but vital distinctions. An *agreement* is not a *contract*, though both are signed, and though *murder* and *manslaughter* are both crimes of killing, they do not carry the same sentence. Distinctions do matter.

3 A parting word from Ogden Nash:

I give you now Professor Twist
A conscientious scientist.
Trustees exclaimed, 'He never bungles!'
And sent him off to distant jungles.
Camped on a tropic riverside,
One day he missed his loving bride.
She had, the guide informed him later,
Been eaten by an alligator.
Professor Twist could not but smile.
'You mean,' he said, 'a crocodile.'

TASK SHEET A   **Definitions**

In the passages below, you will find a number of (possibly)
unfamiliar words for which the writer has offered a brief
explanation or definition. Working with your group, discuss the
explanation of the words in italics and translate the expressions as
accurately as possible. You may, of course, use dictionaries. If you
cannot find the word or expression, suggest one of your own
invention.

1 It is high time the Government implemented its plan to stop
   gazumping. How many families have suffered as a result of this
   dishonest and frustrating practice? Our own editor has received
   hundreds of distressed letters from disappointed couples . . .
   (*Property News*)

2 She looked at me pensively. 'Normality,' she said, 'has a lot to
   recommend it. We take our senses so much for granted. Can you
   imagine what it would be like not to be able to smell? How would
   you feel about food, flowers, bonfires on autumn evenings . . .?
   Just think what you'd be missing.'
   She resumed her 'professional' voice. 'Do you know, thousands of
   people lose the sense of smell every year. *The phenomenon is known
   medically as 'anosmia'*. Of course, some people are born without a
   sense of smell, although *non-congenital anosmia* is uncommon.'
   (Ann Fuller: *My Daughter the Doctor*)

3 Two scientists at the University of California have moved a
   collection of monkeys and other forest and jungle creatures from
   their natural haunts in the tropics to find out more about the
   evolution of *circadian rhythms* in primates and tropical beasts.
   Circadian rhythms are the internal reflection of the Earth's 24–
   hour cycle in the animal, and are surprisingly stable around 24
   hours even when animals are kept in continuous light or
   continuous darkness.
   (*New Scientist*)

4 If you were to place a human brain on a table in front of you, you
   would notice that it is divided neatly into two halves vertically
   from front to back: these are the right and left *cerebral
   hemispheres*. And each hemisphere is further divided into four so-
   called *lobes*: the one at the front (*the frontal lobe*) is responsible for
   controlling movement and for some aspects of emotions; *the
   occipital lobe* (at the back) deals with sight; the lobe at the side
   (*the temporal lobe*) is an important memory store; and *the parietal
   lobe* (at the top) has a vital role in comparing and integrating
   information that flows into the brain through the sensory
   channels of vision, hearing, smell and touch.
   (Richard Leakey and Roger Lewin: *People of the Lake*)

TASK SHEET B   **Definitions**

In the passages below, you will find a number of (possibly) unfamiliar words for which the writer has offered a brief explanation or definition. Working with your group, discuss the explanation of the words in italics and translate the expressions as accurately as possible. You may, of course, use dictionaries. If you cannot find the word or expression, suggest one of your own invention.

1 Concrete must be '*cured*' or kept moist for a period after placing so that the water it contains can complete the chemical action taking place as the concrete hardens. If the concrete dries out too quickly, surface cracks will appear which may affect its effective life.
(J. T. Bowyer: *Small Works Supervision*)

2 Nowadays there is an activity in several cities including New York known as '*rubbling*'. It means the rescuing of decorative sculpture from buildings about to be torn down.
(*The Architectural Review*)

3 Local police in a number of areas have been carrying out research to prevent road accidents that result from driver fatigue. A recent medical briefing in *The Times* reported that the police in Devon had instigated physical training to help tired drivers to stay awake on long car journeys. The results so far look promising, except in the case of one group of drivers whose concentration cannot be restored without sleep. These are *narcoleptics,* who suffer from sudden attacks of sleepiness. *Narcolepsy* and its association with *transient paralysis, sleep paralysis,* and *double vision* was first studied and reported in the medical literature towards the end of the nineteenth century.
(*The Medical Weekly*)

TASK SHEET C   **Distinctions**

In the passages below, your attention is drawn to distinctions – often very fine distinctions – between particular words or concepts. For instance, *tiredness/fatigue, nakedness/nudity.* How would you convey these distinctions in your own language?

1 Sleep is not a necessary result of excessive fatigue. *Tiredness* and *fatigue* are not by any means synonymous. We may feel *tired* and *sleepy* without being unduly *fatigued,* and we may be excessively fatigued without being in any way sleepy.
(C. J. Adcock: *Fundamentals of Psychology*)

2 Consider Mr Smith. He works on an assembly line. He finds the work *dull and tedious*. One day he decides he has had enough and would like just a few days at home. He presents himself to the doctor. The doctor may say, 'Yes, you ought to have a few days off,' and then add a diagnostic tag, such as *stress* or *overwork*. Smith then gets his sick note.

Or the doctor may say, 'There's nothing the matter with you.' His note may read: 'Another *malingerer*'. What process is involved here? What sort of term is *malingering*? It involves a judgement that Smith ought to be working, and that the doctor is not going to aid him in avoiding this responsibility.
(*The Listener*)

3 We can now begin to see the difference between *nakedness* and *nudity* . . . In his book on *The Nude*, Kenneth Clark maintains that to be *naked* is simply to be *without clothes*, whereas *the nude is a form of art*.
(John Berger: *Ways of Seeing*)

4 I had thought I was the only foreigner on the train. I was wrong. I should have known the moment I saw his cut-off dungarees, his full beard, his ear-ring, his maps and rucksack, that he was a fellow-traveller.

He looked contemptuously at my drip-dry shirt, my leakproof shoes, my sunglasses.
'You're a *tourist*?' he said.
'Like you,' I said in a friendly way.
'I am *travelling*,' he said, *forcing the distinction*.
'Five months I have been travelling! Five. I left Paris in October. I spent one month in New York City.'
'*Travelling* in New York City?' This stung him.
(Paul Theroux: *The Old Patagonian Express*)

TASK SHEET D   **Distinctions**

In the passages below, your attention is drawn to distinctions – often very fine distinctions – between particular words or concepts. For instance, *safety/security*, *traveller/tourist*. How would you convey these distinctions in your own language?

1 *Safety and security* are synonymous in most everyday speech – a dictionary defines security as *something that ensures safety*. Notwithstanding that definition, with reference to the doors and windows of a building *safety* has a meaning not only different to

security but possibly in conflict with it. Leaving aside structural safety, *safety* in a building means *protecting users from accidents and disease; security means protecting users from violence, and protecting the contents from thieves and vandals*. One of the sharpest areas of conflicts between the two aims arises from the confrontation of the *safety requirement* of making exit easy in case of fire with the *security requirement* of making entrance difficult to the unauthorised.
(*Building Design*)

2 The Russian-language tourist brochure produced by Essex County Council for Soviet seamen who come ashore at Tilbury has had to be rewritten. The first draft invited them to '*escape to Essex*', with predictable results. The brochure now merely suggests that they '*explore beautiful Essex.*'
(*The Essex Clarion*)

3 With the real travel snobs I have shuddered at the mention of pleasure cruises or circular tours or personally conducted parties, of professional guides and hotels under English management. Every Englishman abroad, until it is proved to the contrary, likes to consider himself *a traveller* and not *a tourist*. As I watched my luggage being lifted onto the 'Stella' I knew that it was no use keeping up the pretence any longer. My fellow passengers and I were *tourists*, without any compromise or extenuation; but we were tourists of a new kind.
(Evelyn Waugh: *Labels*)

4.3 Choice of words: word play

PREPARATION

1 Make a selection of short comments and quotations which include some form of definition, for example: *A diplomat is a man of honour sent abroad to lie for his country.*

2 Prepare a task sheet and make a copy for everyone in the class.

IN CLASS

Ask the students to work in groups of three on the definitions in the task sheet (examples are given in the task sheet at the end of this activity). Set a time-limit of ten to twelve minutes. Each group should translate as many of the definitions as they can within the time. When the time is up, they compare translations.

COMMENTS

This is basically intended as a warm-up activity, or for unwinding. It could also be used with many of the activities in section 2.

TASK SHEET

Below is a selection of 'pithy comments' on various topics. Imagine that you have found them quoted in texts you are working on. How would you translate them?

1 A serious writer is not to be confounded with a solemn writer.
(Ernest Hemingway)

2 Everybody complains of his memory, but nobody of his judgement.
(La Rochefoucauld)

3 No man is a hypocrite in his pleasures.
(Dr Johnson)

4 At a dinner party one should eat wisely but not too well, and talk well but not too wisely.
(Somerset Maugham)

5 A critic is a man who knows the way, but can't drive a car.
(Kenneth Tynan)

6 Asking a working writer what he thinks about critics is like asking a lamp-post how it feels about dogs.
(Christopher Hampton)

7 A bore is a person who talks when you wish him to listen.
(Ambrose Bierce)

8 There is a great difference between a man who does not want to sin and one who does not know how to.
(Seneca)

9 Money is the root of all evil.
(proverb)
The lack of money is the root of all evil.
(George Bernard Shaw)
Money is the root of all evil, and man needs roots.
(John Peers)

10 Dr Johnson (to the Abbess of a convent): 'Madam, you are not here for the love of virtue, but the fear of vice.'
(Boswell)

11 Continental people have sex life; the English have hot-water bottles.
(George Mikes)

12 In 1960 an anecdote in the form of an imaginary dialogue circulated in the satellite countries of the East:
'Tell me, comrade, what is capitalism?'
'The exploitation of man by man.'
'And what is communism?'
'The reverse.'
(Arthur Koestler)

4.4 Possibility and ability

1 Choose passages illustrating various common ways of expressing the notion of *can* in its two main meanings: *to be possible* and *to be able*.

2 Prepare two task sheets, A and B, and make enough copies for half the class.

1 As an introductory activity, review with the whole class the language associated with possibility and ability, both in English and in the mother tongue. There are several ways in which this can be done. Two are described below.

a. Write up two or three short sentences which can be easily transformed, such as:
   - *The seats can be adjusted.*
     It is possible to adjust the seats.
     You/one can adjust the seats.
     The seats are adjustable.

   - *This ticket offers you the possibility of breaking your journey.*
     With this ticket you can break your journey.
     This ticket enables you to break your journey.
     This ticket allows for journeys to be broken.

   - *We could not get any information.*
     There was no information available.
     No information could be obtained.
     It was impossible to get any information.

   The students suggest similar transformations in the mother tongue. They should also explain in what context they would expect the expressions to be used.

b. Write up a list of fifteen to twenty familiar words ending in *–ible/able*. And beneath them, sentences or language fragments in which these words might occur with positive or negative meanings. For instance:

(non–	obtainable	debatable
not	deductible	eligible
un	acceptable	transportable
in	beatable	soluble
ir)	inflammable	regrettable
	edible	workable
	laudible	audible
	changeable	comparable
	available	questionable
	reversible	

   1 (Weather) The outlook is . . . .
   2 The committee has come up with what it hopes is a . . . solution.

3 Beware! Highly . . .!

4 Imported Oriental rugs and carpets at . . . prices!

5 All bills must be paid in local currency or by travellers' cheque. No other form of payment is . . . .

6 The White House spokesman regretted that he was not . . . for comment.

7 For foreign nationals working in the country, tax will be . . . at source.

8 All persons over the age of 65 are . . . for the Senior Citizens' Railcard.

9 (Airline catering) Most major airlines are now replacing glass bottles with lightweight . . . containers.

2 In pairs, the students work on either of the task sheets. They discuss the phrases in italics, and note down their translations of each.

3 They then compare and discuss their versions with other pairs who have worked on the same task sheet.

4 When they have done this, they should exchange task sheets and translate the fresh material as before, and follow up with discussion and comparison between the pairs who have exchanged task sheets.

COMMENTS

1 Concepts such as that of possibility are not strictly definable. Some expressions, such as *can/be able to, enable, facilitate, make possible,* etc. are all, clearly, closely associated. But what about words such as *potential, eventually, opportunity, efficiency* . . .? They too belong, even though the connection with possibility may be less obvious.

Because we are exploring an area which cannot be clearly defined – but which certainly exists – we need a flexible approach. This is why the introductory activity is longer than usual. The students need time to think around the subject, or to explore the area.

2 An excellent way of introducing the topic (in step 1) would be to use the set of variations on a sentence given by Peter Newmark in his book *Approaches to Translation,* and quoted below.

Let me now return to another aspect of synonymy, synonyms in grammar, which are often closer and more numerous than in lexis. Take the German sentence: *Es ist unmöglich, das Problem zu lösen.* We have the following potential translations:

1 It is impossible to resolve the problem.

2 Solving the problem is impossible.

3 The problem is impossible to solve.

4 One cannot solve the problem.

5 A solution to the problem is impossible.

6 The problem is insoluble.

7 To solve the problem is impossible.

8 There is no solution to the problem.

9 The problem has no solution.

10 Solving the problem is an impossibility.

3 Possible wording for the sentences in *In Class*, step 1b:
  1 The outlook is *changeable*.
  2 . . . a *workable* solution.
  3 Highly *inflammable*!
  4 . . . at *unbeatable* prices!
  5 No other form of payment is *acceptable*.
  6 . . . not *available* for comment.
  7 . . . *deductible* at source.
  8 . . . persons over the age of 65 are *eligible* . . .
  9 . . . lightweight *disposable* containers.

TASK SHEET A

Discuss how you would translate the expressions in italics in the texts below.

1 On Translating

'The fact that *we are able to produce an equivalent* in English for every word in a foreign language text does not mean that *we can give an adequate translation* of the text. Translation implies that *we have the capacity* to enter into the mind, the world, and the culture of the speakers or writers and that *we can express their thought* in a manner that is not only parallel to the original, but also acceptable to the target language. *Nearly all language is translatable.* Even *abstruse poetry can often be made as intelligible in another language as it is in the original;* while cultural references, proverbs, idioms, and jokes can at least be replaced by equivalents which carry a message that is conceptually identical in both languages.'
(interview with translator Frederick Fuller)

2 I am quite *incapable of doing any work*, even if the doctors would allow me to, and in fact I have hardly set pen to paper since last December.
(George Orwell: *Collected Essays*)

3 It would appear that children *are capable at an early age* of some differentiation of colour, as of pattern.
(M. D. Vernon: *The Psychology of Perception*)

4 The conventional chair forces your lower back forward, piling unnecessary strain on your spine and back muscles. The 'Back Chair' *allows you to sit up comfortably and naturally*, with spine and back muscles in perfect alignment.
(advertisement)

5 The main auditorium will accommodate 1300 delegates, but sliding dividing walls *will enable the area to be divided* into three, with seating for 300, 600, and 400 people. This development *will provide an opportunity* to build a new entrance at the rear of the Caledonian Hotel.
(*Building Design*)

TASK SHEET B   Discuss how you would translate the expressions in italics in the texts below.

1 **Reading**

There is no doubt that adults vary greatly in *the speed and efficiency* of their reading. Some proceed very slowly; others dash along too quickly and then have to regress. Poor readers in particular *may lack the ability* to vary their manner of reading according to the type of reading matter and their intentions in reading it. A good reader *can move at great speed* through the text. *He may be able to skim a page,* picking up a word or two here and there, and gain a general idea of what the text is about without really reading it. A less efficient reader tends to maintain the same speed whatever the material he reads.
(M. D. Vernon: *The Psychology of Perception*)

2 This is not a car ferry, although *it can convey* bicycles and light motor cycles at the operator's discretion.
(Scottish Tourist Board brochure)

3 Human babies *can swim* when only a few weeks old. If placed in the water, they make reflex swimming movements which actually propel them forward. *This remarkable ability* soon fades. Only children whose experience of swimming is limited to brief annual holidays at the seaside are frightened of the water. Any child living near the sea *can become a proficient swimmer* and diver by the age of five years, and should then *be capable of picking up* small objects from several feet below the water.
(Desmond Morris: *Manwatching*)

4 You *can also use your Access Card* in the Rapid Cash Tills in many of our larger branches. *Any sum up to £50 can be withdrawn* during banking hours.
(National Westminster Bank brochure)

5 Toxic fumes create a film over the eyes, so that *a passenger cannot see* to escape from a burning plane. Passengers are blinded before they choke on the fumes. A smoke hood – or the alternative, a filter mask – *enables passengers* to survive for longer in toxic fumes.
(*New Scientist*)

4.5 Causality: consequence, effect, and result

PREPARATION   1 Try to find short passages containing expressions (mainly verbal) associated with the notion of causality, that is, making things happen or change their state, influencing behaviour, bringing about change, and so on. For example:

– Grit in the petrol was *causing* the car *to stall*.
– The clumsy compliment *made her* only more *angry*.
– Treatment with linseed oil *renders the wood more resistant* to the drying-out effect of sun and wind.

2 Prepare two sets of task sheets, A and B, and make enough copies for half the class.

3 An optional text for further work (task sheet C) is given at the end of this activity.

IN CLASS

1 As a warm-up, write up five or six sentences similar to the ones above. Here are three more:

– Particular colours may *give rise to* particular emotional *reactions*: red to excitement or anger, black and grey to sadness or depression.
– *The drought* in Timbuktu *has been caused by* a permanent shift in climate.
– If you have any complaints, please let us know. We want to *make your stay as enjoyable as possible*.

Ask the class as a whole to suggest at least two translations for each of these sentences. Note on the board the various renderings of the expressions in italics. (More expressions will be added to this list at the end of the activity.)

2 Ask the students to work in groups of three, half the class using task sheet A, half task sheet B. They should translate the passages orally, but should keep a note of all suggestions offered for the expressions in italics.

3 When they have finished, the groups exchange task sheets and notes. They now translate their new sets, as before. They then compare their own suggestions with those given by the previous group. Any questions or doubts should be cleared up in discussion.

4 General discussion: The students now add to the list of L1 expressions on the board by selecting key phrases from the sets they have worked on. Discuss in particular any expressions which are similar in English but may be different in translation, for example:

– the child . . . *causes things to move*
– the fact that something has happened a number of times *causes animals and men to expect* . . .

5 (Optional) The students may like to discuss fields of association, both in English and in the mother tongue. (Some suggestions are given at the end of *Comments*.)

COMMENTS

1 I have suggested doing this mainly as an oral activity in order to give the students time to cover a wider range of examples. This will allow them to compare structures and to see more clearly any general patterns which emerge. The note-taking is a device to prevent the oral translation from becoming too loose: writing down their translations of the words in italics makes the students think precisely about how these expressions fit into the overall structure.

2 One of the main purposes of the activity is to make students aware of the options open to them in their own language for expressing the very familiar concept of causality. Most languages will have a range of possibilities, some of which may seem to match the English (*rendre, causer, créer, provoquer, avoir comme suite*), but will not necessarily match in the same contexts. What we are exploring here is how and where the two systems overlap, and where they differ.

3 Further work might be done on constructions with *make* (*make difficult, make audible, make (to) move*). In spite of their importance, I have not treated them as a separate category because, for the translator, they belong together with other ways of expressing causality.

4 Below, for reference, is a check-list of some of the commonest expressions associated with causality.
- *make* + verb, noun, adjective (*make difficulties, make* (to) *move, make easier*)
- *cause* (rapid drying will *cause cracks to appear*)
- *bring about / lead to* (inflation has *brought about / led to* great changes in living standards)

A number of other verbs also express causality:
- *create*
- *produce*
- *provoke*
- *give rise to*
- *force / oblige*

- *render*
- *change / alter*
- *diminish / increase*
- *worsen / improve*

and verbs ending in *-ize / ise, -ify:*
- *dramatize*
- *neutralize*
- *sterilize*
  etc.

- *magnify*
- *amplify*
- *purify*

TASK SHEET A

Translate the following passages orally, but note down the various renderings of the expressions in italics. Wherever possible, suggest two (or more) translations for each expression.

1 Detailed calculations find that the acceleration of an object under gravity depends on both the mass and temperature of an object in a way that *makes heavier, or cooler objects fall faster* than lighter or hotter ones.
(*The Listener*)

2 The job of the typographer is to *make the reading* of the printed page *easy and pleasant*, and in illustrated books to *make sure that*, for example, *the connection* between text and illustrations *is clear*.
(*The Author*)

3 To be a good teacher, you need to *make the material varied; interesting,* and *understandable* to your students.
(*New Methodology*)

4 Although Miss Quested had not *made herself popular* with the English, she brought out all that was fine in their character.
(E. M. Forster: *A Passage to India*)

5 Probably the child first becomes aware of causality when he himself *causes things to move* by pushing, pulling, and shaking them. Such movements occur at first by chance, and then the child *begins to produce them intentionally.* Thus one of Piaget's children found at the age of three months that by kicking around in her cot she could *make her dolls,* which were suspended from a framework above the cot, *move to and fro.*
(M. D. Vernon: *The Psychology of Perception*)

6 The mere fact that something has happened a certain number of times *causes animals and men to expect* that it will happen again. Thus our instincts certainly *cause us to believe* that the sun will rise tomorrow.
(Bertrand Russell: *Problems of Philosophy*)

7 (In India) To send a telegram in the ordinary public fashion *necessitates at least four separate but interrelated operations.* First, you approach the counter, which is besieged by a shrilling, gesticulating crowd . . .
(James Cameron: *An Indian Summer*)

TASK SHEET B Translate the following passages orally, but note down the various renderings of the expressions in italics. Wherever possible, suggest two (or more) translations for each expression.

1 Gandhi was released from prison early in 1924. Almost his first public act was a three-week fast in the cause of communal unity. This *led to a conference* on unity, and once more he was in the centre of affairs.
(Percival Spear: *A History of India*)

2 Mrs Thatcher has succeeded in *making people believe* in her economic 'miracle', which, as we have repeatedly argued, is largely an illusion.
(*The Economic Review*)

3 As one delegate to the Cannes film festival put it: 'Technically the British are always superb, but when you are watching a comedy show only one question really counts – *does it make you laugh?*'
(*Arts Weekly*)

4 It is not surprising to find that success or failure in a task *has some effect on the performance of that task* itself, and *may also affect tasks* performed immediately afterwards.
(M. D. Vernon: *The Psychology of Perception*)

5 Make-up does several things to the human face. It may disguise it or protect it from the sun; it may *make it look younger and healthier*, or it may label it as belonging to a particular social category.
(Desmond Morris: *Manwatching*)

6 You can lead a horse to water, but you can't *make him drink*.
(popular saying)

7 A type of reading *which necessitates careful attention* to detail is proof-reading, in which the reader, in order to detect misprints, has to notice not so much the meaning of what he reads as the exact shapes and order of letters and words in the text.
(M. D. Vernon: *The Psychology of Perception*)

8 In any interaction which *makes you anxious*, you can learn to adjust your own body language and feel more confident. Try to avoid wringing your hands, as this conveys nervousness, or raising your forefinger when you speak because the implicit aggression *will arouse an unco-operative response*.
(*SHE* magazine)

TASK SHEET C

Translate the passage below, paying special attention to the words in italics.

Immunotoxins

The administration of active toxins to an animal or person will probably *produce adverse side effects* because the poison kills normal cells as well. It would be a good idea *if we could modify the toxins* so that they kill only cancer cells. One way is to attach these toxins to substances called antibodies, which *react specifically with tumour cells to produce 'immunotoxins'*. Antibodies are protein molecules *produced by animals, in response to* a foreign substance, or antigen. Antibodies combine specifically with the substance *that induced their formation*. In this case, specific active molecules on the surface of the cancer cells *trigger the formation* of antibodies. Therefore, in theory, the immunotoxin will selectively seek out and kill the tumour cell.

(*New Scientist*)

4.6 Perception: seeing and understanding

1 Select passages relating to *seeing* in both the literal and the figurative sense (physical perception and mental comprehension). Key words in the passages would be, for instance: *grasp, see, perceive, appreciate, realize; recognition, realization, awareness, perception* . . .

2 Prepare two sets of task sheets, A and B, and make enough copies for half the class.

3 You may wish to prepare an OHT (see *In class*, step 5).

4 An additional text for further work (task sheet C) is given at the end of this activity.

1 As a warm-up, present the students with two or three short sentences which could be easily varied in wording, such as:

I showed her the original picture and the copy . . .
– and she *saw* the difference at once.
– but she could *perceive* no difference.
– but she *did not appreciate* the difference.
– but she *was not aware* of any difference.
– but she *realized* at once which must be the copy.
– and she *recognized* the original without any difficulty.
– but she *did not notice* that they were different.

2 Before inviting translations, ask the students to consider in which sentences they think the picture is looked at slowly or quickly, the person showing the picture might also offer an explanation, the viewer has seen at least one of the pictures before, etc.

The students should try to translate each variant in several ways. But they may, of course, use the same expressions in different sentences (*was not aware / did not notice* might both be translated as *elle n'a pas remarqué*).

3 Ask the students to work in groups of three on the passages in the task sheets. The translation should be done orally, but all variants for the expressions in italics should be noted down.

4 When ready, each group exchanges task sheets and notes with another. They translate, as before, and then compare their suggestions with the notes they received from the previous group.

5 Follow this up with a group discussion. Since there will probably be no time to discuss each example in detail, an economical way of summarizing the work would be to write up only the key words from each passage (*perceive, awareness, consciousness of*). These could be prepared in advance on an OHP transparency, or on the back of the blackboard (if it is movable!), on these lines:

Task sheet A

1 *seeing, look at, aware, sight*
2 *consciously, knowledge, consciousness, observe, aware*
3 *perceiving, appear, sight, sight*
  etc.

Task sheet B

1 *perceive, visual, look*
2 *unaware, aware*
3 *see, sees*
  etc.

Next to each item, write in the different words or constructions suggested. This will help to reveal, though crudely, to what extent the English expressions overlap with those of the L1, and where the differences lie.

COMMENTS

1 Because the language we are dealing with here is so familiar, some students may think the activity too easy, or find the range too limited. Certainly, it should not be difficult to translate the examples. But the challenge is to translate them accurately and, in so doing, to explore the full potential of the mother tongue with regard to a concept which will occur, in one form or another, on almost any written page. The concept may be familiar, but familiarity should not breed contempt.

2 A useful task (for private work), which can be based on the activities in this section, is to keep a record from your reading of SL expressions relating to concepts and notions. In addition to *possibility, cause and result,* and *seeing/understanding,* some of the most important – for the translator – include:

– expressing doubt, disagreement, disapproval
– stating opinions (*It is my belief, I consider,* etc.)
– giving instructions
– expressing certainty
– speaking of expectations (anticipations, hopes, etc.)

3 Finally, a language practice activity which is also relevant to translation, is to take a single word or expression in English and present it in several different contexts:

– I *noticed* him just as he was turning the corner.
– I *noticed that* he was in a bad mood.
– Next morning *we noticed* the outlines of an island.
– *Notice* the detail at the centre of the mosaic.

These should be translated, where possible, by different expressions in the L1.

TASK SHEET A

In the passages below, the expressions in italics all relate, in some way, to *seeing*. This may be seeing in the physical sense (*observe, perceive*) or in the sense of understanding (*appreciate, be aware*).

Without using a dictionary, translate the passages orally, but note down all suggestions for the expressions in italics.

1 Every image embodies *a way of seeing*. Even a photograph. Every time we *look at* a photograph, we *are aware*, however slightly, of the photographer selecting *that sight* from an infinity of other possible sights.
(John Berger: *Ways of Seeing*)

2 Can we *consciously* control a reflex? Obviously some at least cannot be controlled since they operate *without our knowledge. We have no consciousness* of the changes in size of our pupils *unless we observe our eyes* in a mirror. In other cases *we are aware* of the response but not until after it takes place, as in the case of withdrawal reflexes.
(C. J. Adcock: *Fundamentals of Psychology*)

3 All thinking is sorting, classifying. All *perceiving* relates to expectations and therefore to comparisons. When we say that from the air *houses appear like toys to us* we mean, I suggest, that we are startled by the *unfamiliar sight* of a house that compares to the *familiar sight* of a toy on the nursery floor.
(E. H. Gombrich: *Art and Illusion*)

4 The architects have succeeded in preserving the character of the (original) building by keeping all the existing window openings and most of the shutters. The structure of the building is *most easily appreciated* at lower ground-floor level.
(*Architectural Review*)

5 'Would you like a letter about this arrangement?' the Minister finally suggested. Anything to clear up the confusion, I thought. 'Yes please, Your Highness.'
'Perhaps you would like to draft the letter for me to sign?' he said.
Suddenly it dawned on me. With the backing of the Sultan Qaboos, the Ministry of Culture was offering to pay for the entire cost of my Sindbad voyage.
(Tim Severin: *The Sindbad Voyage*)

6 Since it is an essential character of prejudice that its sources are hidden from *consciousness*, it might seem to be impossible for us *to become aware* of our own prejudices so that we may become free from their influence.
(Robert Thouless: *Straight and Crooked Thinking*)

TASK SHEET B

In the passages below, the expressions in italics all relate, in some way, to *seeing*. This may be seeing in the physical sense (*perceive*) or in the sense of understanding (*recognize, appreciate, be aware*).

Without using a dictionary, translate the passages orally, but note down all suggestions for the expressions in italics.

1 Sometimes an observer may wish *to perceive* what is happening at several points *in the visual field*; for instance, the readings of instrument dials and gauges on an instrument panel. In this case *he must look* rapidly to and fro, from one to another.
(M. D. Vernon: *The Psychology of Perception*)

2 One of the difficulties with faulty body language is that *we are usually unaware* of what our faces or hands or shoulders are doing because these body patterns have become automatic. *We only become aware of them* when they are pointed out to us.
(*SHE* magazine)

3 Painting is an activity, and the artist will therefore tend to *see what he paints* rather than to *paint what he sees*.
(E. H. Gombrich: *Art and Illusion*)

4 One quality in the world *that is appreciated* by the human mind is the passage of time. *A true perception* of events in the outside world is impossible unless time is automatically built into the analysis of information about them. In this sense any animal that is *dealing with a perceptual world* of even a small degree of complexity must have a brain capable of comparing events in the context of time as well as in space. But *the appreciation of time* is quite separate from this.
(Richard Leakey and Roger Lewin: *People of the Lake*)

5 'I've brought an old friend to see you,' repeated Stroeve. Strickland looked at me thoughtfully for nearly a minute. I did not speak.
'I've never seem him in my life,' he said.
I do not know why he said this, for I felt certain I had caught *a gleam of recognition* in his eyes.
(Somerset Maugham: *The Moon and Sixpence*)

KEY TO TASK C

Original wording:

1 b) sensory	6 c) consciously
2 a) deteriorates	7 a) attention
3 a) reduced	8 b) being conscious
4 c) unaware	9 a) look at
5 c) habitual	

TASK SHEET C In the passage below, certain words have been left out. From the choices given at the end, select the word you consider most appropriate in each case.

Attention and Perception

We must conclude that normal consciousness, perception, and thought can be maintained only in a constantly changing environment. When there is no change, a state of (1) ' . . . deprivation' occurs; the capacity of adults to concentrate (2) . . ., attention fluctuates and lapses, and normal perception fades.

Even when attention is (3) . . ., and perception becomes so unclear that we are uncertain as to what we perceive, or indeed may be (4) . . . that we perceive anything, nevertheless some degree of marginal awareness may persist. Moreover, in much of our (5) . . . and automatic behaviour it is clear that we do indeed perceive our surroundings and are able to react to them appropriately without being (6) . . . aware of what is present. Thus we cannot equate perception or even attention with consciousness. Perception may occur at a very low level of (7) . . ., when awareness is marginal and not fully conscious. In some cases we may become conscious that we remember certain events after they occurred, without having attended to them or been fully aware of them at the time.

But we also have evidence of cases in which people have apparently perceived things without ever (8) . . . that they did so. In one of the first experiments carried out on this phenomenon, observers were shown coloured shapes resembling a banana, an orange, a lemon, and a leaf, in a very dim light. They were told to (9) . . . the screen on which these shapes were projected, and at the same time imagine each of them in turn. They then thought that what appeared was in fact a visual image, and were not conscious that they perceived the image at all. However, if they were instructed beforehand that they would perceive these objects, they did so normally.

(M. D. Vernon: *The Psychology of Perception*)

1 a) cognitive   b) sensory   c) intellectual
2 a) deteriorates   b) decreases   c) diminishes
3 a) reduced   b) decreased   c) diminished
4 a) unsure   b) unconscious   c) unaware
5 a) unconscious   b) reflex   c) habitual
6 a) fully   b) actively   c) consciously
7 a) attention   b) awareness   c) consciousness
8 a) realizing   b) being conscious   c) noticing   d) being aware
9 a) look at   b) concentrate on   c) observe

"Brilliant technique but he has nothing to say"

5 Idiom: from one culture to another

Idiom *n*. Language of a people or country; specific character of this; form of expression peculiar to a language or person, peculiarity of phraseology approved by usage though having meaning not deducible from those of the separate words; characteristic mode of expression in music, art, etc.

(*The Concise Oxford Dictionary*)

Introduction

This section brings the book full circle. Indeed, it takes us right back to the point from which we began – context and register – but from a different approach. While in the previous four sections we were concerned primarily with language, with the transfer from one language to another, here we concentrate rather on expression, on the transfer from one culture to another.

The theme of this section could be summarized, very briefly, as: questions that lie beyond the dictionary. That is, questions that cannot be solved merely by translating the surface meaning. Here we will be exploring what lies behind the words: tone, innuendo, implication, hidden reference, irony, metaphor, imagery – all those features of language which need to be not only translated but also interpreted.

An example may help to make this clear. In a tourist brochure we may read:

> Hotel Adriatic: a popular 1st class hotel overlooking the harbour with fine views of the local islands and Hvar town. One bar, two lounges, terrace restaurant, indoor sea-water pool and sun terrace on top floor.

In a play we may read:

> The old Edwardian brigade do make their brief little world look pretty tempting. Always the same picture: high summer, the long days in the sun, slim volumes of verse, crisp linen, the smell of starch.

On the face of it, there is no problem in either text that could not be solved by reference to a dictionary. So, *fine views of the local islands* or *slim volumes of verse* should, in principle, give the translator no difficulty. But what the dictionary may not tell the translator is that 'slim volumes' is ironic, while 'fine views' is not; that the phrase 'slim volumes' suggests genteel, refined tasks, that it is associated with a certain period, a certain class of people, and a way of life, and that the expression is slightly archaic. Clearly, 'slim volume' would not be the same in English as 'thin book' or 'short volume'. In such a case, a faithful translation of the words might be an unfaithful interpretation of the meaning.

Translation is 'crossing the border' from one language to another. The questions which lie beyond the dictionary lie on both sides of the border.

Outline of this section

There is, in all the activities, a strong emphasis on the spoken language, or speech in writing. This is partly because a section on *Idiom* cannot ignore the influence of the spoken language on the written – an influence which is much less felt in the reverse direction! But another, and most important reason, is that the use of translation, as a language learning activity, tends to be associated exclusively with the written word. Yet translation and interpreting, as professional activities, are closely associated with the spoken word or, at the very least, with speech in writing.

The texts offered for translation in class are not always those offered in the market-place. What the market offers is not (usually) the essays of Hazlitt, Ruskin, or Lamb, but cartoons, cheap thrillers, instructions for washing machines, abstracts for scientific articles, business letters, interviews, documentary films, conference programmes, and introductions to catalogues. Much of this material will contain a mixture of spoken and written language. In addition, it may also be badly worded, badly presented, and needed in a hurry.

This is why this section begins with *The translator and the text*, a brief exercise in practical criticism.

From here we move on to what might be called 'formula language', which includes familiar or 'fixed' expressions, cliché, jargon, 'dead metaphor', etc., in activity 5.3.

The activity that follows, *Colloquialisms*, completes the circle, and brings us back to section 1, the difference being that here the students are required not just to translate idiomatic expressions but also to interpret their meaning in terms of their own culture.

The last five activities review the question that runs right through the book: *How would I say this in my own language?*, and are designed to give the students a foretaste of the kind of work they might be expected to do in the life that goes on – outside the classroom.

5.1 The translator and the text: defective and ambiguous sentences

PREPARATION

1 Try to find sentences which are inaccurate, unclear or ambiguous, or which contain a defect which might easily be carried over into a translation, as in:

> The catching and eating of other animals is by no means the sole diet of a wild carnivore.

The wording is inaccurate: *catching and eating* is not <u>a diet.</u>

2 Make up two task sheets, A and B, and prepare enough copies for half the class.

IN CLASS

This is basically an oral exercise, which should be done as far as possible in English. No translation is required.

1 Divide the students into groups of three and give half the groups in the class task sheet A, and the other half task sheet B. They should identify in each example where the defect lies, suggest ways in which it could be corrected, and note down their suggestions.

2 When they are ready, each group exchanges task sheets with another group.

3 Follow up the activity with discussion of the problems and of the solutions offered.

COMMENTS

1 Although no translation is involved here, this activity gives practice in a skill vital to the translator: the ability to detect errors and to correct them. Since correcting is usually much harder than detecting, the students may need to be reminded that this is not simply a 'spot the error' game.

2 The *Notes* given after the task sheets offer a brief explanation of what I consider the problems to be. They are not exhaustive, and there is room for disagreement.

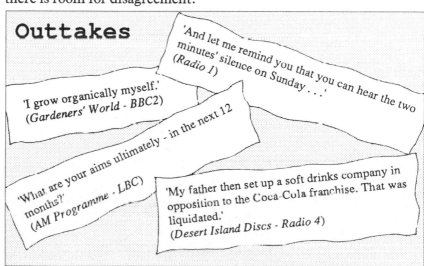

Outtakes

'And let me remind you that you can hear the two minutes' silence on Sunday . . .'
(Radio 1)

'I grow organically myself.'
(Gardeners' World - BBC2)

'What are your aims ultimately - in the next 12 months?'
(AM Programme - LBC)

'My father then set up a soft drinks company in opposition to the Coca-Cola franchise. That was liquidated.'
(Desert Island Discs - Radio 4)

TASK SHEET A

In the short passages below, you will find sentences which could be misunderstood (or mistranslated) because they are ambiguous. Decide where the defects lie and, if possible, correct them.

1 Economic development in New Zealand has not been achieved, as in most market-oriented economies, through an emphasis on industrialization.

2 Bolivia, it appears, has now become the cocaine capital of the world, cannot exist without it, and supplies more than half the needs of the booming American drug market.

3 The catching and eating of other animals is by no means the sole diet of a wild carnivore. A variety of plant matters from roots to bark, leaves, and even fruit is eaten.

4 The keen reader of Hardy's novels on a visit to Dorset will recognize many of the places mentioned in the novels and are little altered since the period he describes.

5 Emotion is running high at the moment, but that emotion must not be allowed to temper sensible judgement.

6 The (British) Government makes little effort to tap European Community Funds for training women because they discriminate against men, according to the Department of Employment.

TASK SHEET B

In the short passages below, you will find sentences which could be misunderstood (or mistranslated) because they are ambiguous. Decide where the defects lie and, if possible, correct them.

1 Being eight years old her question, when it came, was straight to the point.

2 **Furniture and dogs sell well**

He also bought an engaging Neapolitan poodle, painted by an unknown eighteenth century artist with Vesuvius erupting behind his fashionably shaved posterior.

3 Racially prejudiced action by police will not be made a specific disciplinary offence, as recommended by Lord Scarman, the Home Secretary told MPs.

4 You could walk all round St Mary's without encountering barbed wire or 'Keep Off' signs. It is a safe place to bring children and where parents may enjoy peace of mind.

5 Conservatives, unlike their opponents, welcome opposition which is good for the democratic system.

6 WORLD ECONOMY ON THE BRINK OF RECOVERY

NOTES

At the risk of stating the obvious, I offer these brief comments on the examples on the task sheets.

Task sheet A

1 Ambiguous. What is the meaning of *as*? Is it: 'as it *has* been achieved' or 'as it has *not* been achieved in most market-oriented economies'?

2 Incorrect reference. In the expression *cocaine capital*, 'cocaine' functions as an adjective (like 'rubber' in *rubber gloves*). Strictly speaking, *it* refers to *capital*, not to cocaine. Solution: change *it* to *the drug*, or repeat *cocaine*.

3 False connection. A *diet* should refer to the kind of food eaten, not to the way it is obtained. *Catching* and *eating* animals is not a diet. Change to something like 'Animal flesh is by no means the sole diet of a wild carnivore . . .', or 'The diet of a wild carnivore does not consist solely of meat obtained by hunting.'

4 Missing reference: *which*. The writer has taken a short-cut. The wording should be:
The reader of Hardy's novel will recognize many of the places
– *which are* mentioned in the novels and *are* little altered . . .
or
– *mentioned* in the novels, *and little altered* . . .
or
– *mentioned* in the novels, (and) *which are little altered*.

5 Wrong meaning. *To temper* means to 'moderate, restrain, tone down'. The writer has said the opposite of what is meant. The sentence should read, 'Emotion is running . . . but that emotion must not be allowed to *inflame / disturb / upset* sensible judgement.'

6 Ambiguity caused by missing reference. In the phrase 'because *they* discriminate against men . . .', the word *they* does not refer, as one might think it does, to *women*; nor does it refer to EEC *funds*. It in fact refers to EEC *policies*, which are not mentioned.

Task sheet B

1 Loose structure. *Being eight years old* clearly refers to the child, not to the question. I suggest: 'Since she was only eight years old, her question – when it came – was straight to the point', or 'She was eight years old, so her question . . .'

2 Reference/ambiguity. '*His fashionably shaved posterior*' seems to refer to the artist, rather than to the dog. All that is needed is a comma after 'an unknown eighteenth century artist'.

3 Ambiguous. What does *as recommended* mean? Did Lord Scarman recommend, or not recommend, that racially prejudiced action by police should be made a specific disciplinary offence?

4 Missing reference. The second sentence should read: 'It is a safe place to bring children and *one* where parents may enjoy peace of mind'.

5 Ambiguous. Do conservatives welcome *the kind of opposition* which is good for the democratic system, or do they welcome opposition *because* opposition is good for the democratic system?

6 Wrong idiom. The word *brink* is associated, almost exclusively, with *disaster*. The expression should have been: 'On the *verge* of recovery'.

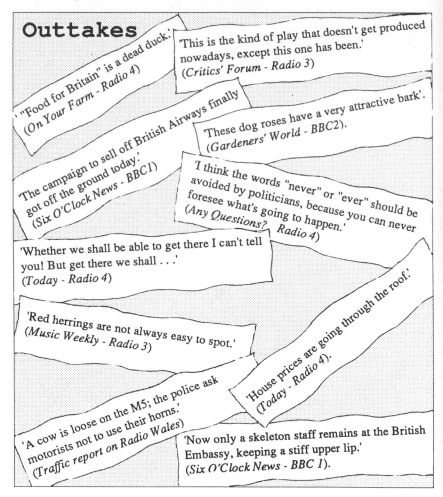

Outtakes

' "Food for Britain" is a dead duck.'
(On Your Farm - Radio 4)

'This is the kind of play that doesn't get produced nowadays, except this one has been.'
(Critics' Forum - Radio 3)

'The campaign to sell off British Airways finally got off the ground today.'
(Six O'Clock News - BBC1)

'These dog roses have a very attractive bark'.
(Gardeners' World - BBC2).

'I think the words "never" or "ever" should be avoided by politicians, because you can never foresee what's going to happen.'
(Any Questions? - Radio 4)

'Whether we shall be able to get there I can't tell you! But get there we shall . . .'
(Today - Radio 4)

'Red herrings are not always easy to spot.'
(Music Weekly - Radio 3)

'House prices are going through the roof.'
(Today - Radio 4).

'A cow is loose on the M5; the police ask motorists not to use their horns.'
(Traffic report on Radio Wales)

'Now only a skeleton staff remains at the British Embassy, keeping a stiff upper lip.'
(Six O'Clock News - BBC 1).

5.2 The translator and the text: choice of words

PREPARATION

1 Try to find passages of translation into English, in which the choice of words would strike an English reader as odd, or at least unexpected. The passages should preferably not have any other distracting errors.

For certain words or expressions, three alternatives are given, one of which is the wording used by the translator.

2 Prepare enough copies of each of the task sheets for one third of the class, or for the whole class if you wish to set a task for out-of-class work.

IN CLASS

The students can work either on the short passages in task sheets A and B, or on the longer text 'The Paris Metro', in task sheet C. An alternative is to set task sheet C for out-of-class work.

1 Before beginning, remind the students that the purpose of this activity is to discuss translations as pieces of writing in English. We do not have the source language text, nor do we need it here. Our concern is not so much with the accuracy as with the quality of the text – as English.

2 Working in pairs or in groups of three, the students discuss the alternatives offered for the missing expressions. In each case, they should rank them in order of preference; for instance, if for task sheet A they write: *1 c, b, a,* it means that *1 c* was the choice most preferred, *1 a* the least.

3 Each pair or group of three then compares notes with another pair working on the same task sheet. They should then move on to a different task sheet for further comparison and discussion.

4 When the students have finished, give them the wording used by the translators.

COMMENTS

1 This is a companion exercise to activity 5.1.

2 Judging a translation without reference to the source language text might seem to be an unusual (and unfair!) activity. But it is not. After all, most of the translations we encounter in daily life reach us without an accompanying SL text. All we have to go by are the translated words. It is important, therefore, to study our own reactions to translation.

Discussing alternatives need not imply criticism of the translator. The activity has a more positive purpose than that, which is to examine the possibilities, to ask 'in what other ways could this same thought be expressed?' This is the question we must ask all the time when we ourselves are translating.

3 I have kept down to the minimum the number of translations into English by non-native speakers. This is because such translations are notoriously difficult to 'correct', for they often involve both structural and idiomatic problems at the same time. Besides, the main concern of this book is with translation from not into English.

However, I realize that many teachers will be equally interested in both. For those who are, some useful ideas may be found in Alan Duff: *The Third Language,* which deals with recurrent problems of translation into English.

TASK SHEET A   The passages below are all taken from translations into English from other languages. For certain expressions, three alternatives are given, one of which was used by the translator. Decide in each case which you think is the best and which the worst of the alternatives.

1 Pure and gentle talcum powder for the care of very sensitive (1) . . .. The components and the (2) . . . fragrance of it are especially indicated for baby's skin.
(advertisement for talcum powder)

   1 a) epidermis   b) bodies   c) skin
   2 a) light   b) slight   c) gentle

2 The organ of the St. George Cathedral Church which is heard on our recording, is the oldest one in Hungary (1) . . . even one of the oldest organs in Central Europe. According to the Payr Chronicle it was (2) . . . in 1633 probably by a Viennese master.
(record sleeve)

   1 a) possibly   b) and maybe   c) but perhaps
   2 a) constructed   b) accomplished   c) made

3 The success of the organization of the Games (1) . . . the fact that it resulted from the concerted teamwork of amateurs.
(report on the 'student Olympics')

   1 a) may be credited to   b) has to be observed in the light of
      c) was clearly due to

TASK SHEET B   The passages below are all taken from translations into English from other languages. For certain expressions, three alternatives are given, one of which was used by the translator. Decide in each case which you think is the best and which the worst of the alternatives.

1 The first autumn days, and tourists in large numbers are leaving the Yugoslav Adriatic to (1) . . .. Still, some 350,000 others, who prefer a more quiet season, (2) . . ..

   1 a) return to the daily grind   b) take their daily jobs again
      c) go back to their daily work
   2 a) can be sure of a good reception from the local hotels
      b) will be well looked after wherever they stay
      c) are cared for by the ever diligent hotel-industry workers

2 In Debrecen today, the relics of the past (1) . . .

   1 a) blend attractively with the modern buildings
     b) are harmoniously integrated with the modern developments
     c) are mingled with the results of modern town development in a pleasant manner

3 Kalemegdan, the oldest part of Belgrade. (1) . . .: Roman bastions, medieval Magyar and Serbian turrets, Ottoman gates, Austrian bulwarks – all this is to be seen here.

   1 a) On this spot it is possible to follow signs of life almost two thousand years old.
     b) Here one may find traces of a past almost two thousand years old.
     c) In this park, one can find remnants of a past dating back almost two thousand years.

KEY TO TASKS

The numbers below indicate the original wording of the translations. My own preference is given in brackets after each.

Task sheet A
1 1a (1c), 2b (2a)
2 1c (1a), 2b (2a)
3 1b (1a)

Task sheet B
1 1b (1a), 2c (2a)
2 1c (1a)
3 1a (1c)

TASK SHEET C

Read the passage below and select, from the alternatives that follow, the words you consider most appropriate for each space.

The Paris Metro

In extending into the inner and outer suburbs, the metro and RER have today (1) . . . the historical gap between Paris and its suburbs, a gap that the metro of the Belle Epoque had helped to accentuate.

In 1950, domicile-work trips represented more than 80% of RATP traffic. At the present time, this percentage is about 50%. By the year 2000, it will probably (2) . . . about 40%. In future years, journeys for 'personal reasons', as statisticians call them, will develop rapidly. When people take the metro to go shopping, to go to the cinema, to see friends, to visit an art exhibition or simply (3) . . . about the Flea Market or the Forum des Halles, they (4) . . . .

However, the environment of the metro was for a long time (5) . . ., designed to (6) . . . . Only the frameworks of glass and cast iron (7) . . . by Hector Guimard for the decoration of metro entrances can be considered as exceptions to this rule. (8) . . . the time spent in this cold and impersonal world of the metro was considered lost time, a temporal gap which people tried, as best they could, to fill by reading a book or scanning a newspaper.

To create a warmer atmosphere, (9) . . . to renovate the stations (9) . . . . More than 100 stations were totally rebuilt. Several of them now bear witness to the past, to the riches and (10) . . . of the neighbourhood they serve. For example, the Louvre station has become a showcase of the famous museum, and the Hotel-de-Ville station recounts the history of the Paris Town Hall.
(Michel Rousselot: 'Le Métro français et la ville', in Air France *Atlas*.)

1 a) bridged   b) eradicated   c) removed   d) closed

2 a) be as low as   b) have dropped to   c) have descended to

3 a) for the purpose of strolling   b) to stroll   c) stroll

4 a) are in a mood to appreciate the attractiveness of their surroundings
  b) feel more open to the impressions around them
  c) find themselves in a mood of the greatest receptivity to environmental influences

5 a) little more than the outer casing of a giant machine
  b) only a simple packaging of a great technological machine
  c) merely a functional 'dressing' for this mechanical marvel

6 a) ensure Parisians journey in the best conditions of rapidity and security
  b) transport passengers as swiftly and safely as possible
  c) provide Paris with safe, rapid public transport

7 a) imagined   b) created   c) conceived   d) designed

8 a) Consequently,   b) Understandably,   c) Result:

9 a) every effort was made (to renovate the stations.)
  b) an important effort (to renovate the stations) was undertaken
  c) the RATP launched a scheme (to renovate the stations.)

10 a) originality   b) the individual character   c) unique features

---

KEY TO TASK C

The text we are dealing with here is a sound translation into English of an article aimed at the general reader. That is, someone who will read the article as if it were a piece of English.

What interests us in the discussion, then, is not whether the translation is accurate (and on the whole, it is), but whether it is clear. The options offered for each blank are intended as thought-provokers. Which of the alternatives offered would you find most satisfactory – in context?

In the scheme below you will find, in first place, the original wording used by the translator. And, in second place (in brackets) my own preference, based on the three alternatives. I must stress that all alternatives are structurally acceptable, and that my preferences are personal choices, not absolute judgements.

1 b (d)	6 a (c)
2 c (b)	7 a (c)
3 a (b)	8 c (b)
4 c (b)	9 b (c)
5 b (c)	10 a (b)

5.3 On the beaten track: familiar expressions

PREPARATION

1 The passages you choose should contain expressions which are 'fixed', or in some way predictable in context. Jargon, cliché, worn-out metaphors and ready-made phrases – all these are appropriate. So too are standard expressions such as: *in the author's opinion, in all probability, . . . remains to be seen,* etc.

2 Prepare two task sheets, A and B, and make enough copies for half the class.

IN CLASS

1 Hand out the task sheets and ask the students to work in groups of three on the examples in your task sheets. For each of the blanks they should choose the alternative they consider most likely to occur in the given context. (One of the alternatives is the expression used in the text.)

In the discussion, they should also decide which of the alternatives is least likely, and why. After noting their decisions, they should exchange sets with another group.

2 The groups work on their second set, as before. When they are ready, they discuss their decisions with the group they exchanged sets with.

COMMENTS

1 In the title of this activity, *On the beaten track*, I have tried to suggest that the emphasis here is not on the quality but on the predictability of language. The students are not being asked to attach labels (*jargon, cliché, dead metaphor,* etc.) to expressions such as *ways and means, aims and objectives,* or *cognitive abilities.* All they are required to do is to pick out the expression they consider most likely to occur in the context.

2 Since the focus of the activity is on the predictability of language (why do we expect, and accept, certain expressions in a particular context?), it is important to encourage the students to discuss their reasons for rejecting any of the alternatives. For instance, why would we expect (in a tourist brochure): 'In Agra, there's more than the Taj *to feast your eyes on*', rather than '*to be considered*'?

These questions can only be answered by picking up clues from the text to tell us which beaten path the writer is following.

3 This task takes us back to the questions raised in activity 1.1.

TASK SHEET A

In each of the passages below, choose the expression you consider most likely to have been used in the original text. The alternatives are given at the end of each passage.

1 One of India's most ancient cities, (1) . . . in legend, is Agra, where mighty empires reached their zenith under the great Mughal dynasty hundreds of years ago. Today, a visit to Agra means to (2) . . . of an empire that has left its imprint on marble and sandstone. Agra is the city of the Taj Mahal, that (3) . . . monument of love which the emperor Shah Jehan built for his queen, Mumtaz Mahal. It is (4) . . . in white marble.
(*A Guide to Agra*)

1 a) noted   b) steeped   c) recorded
2 a) gain an impression   b) appreciate the significance
   c) experience the glory
3 a) immortal   b) notable   c) well-proportioned
4 a) an edifice   b) a dream   c) an architectural triumph

2 The papers presented in this collection report on research indicating that second language learners bring (1) . . . learning skills to the task of acquiring second language competence. They also bring to light the knowledge learners have about (2) . . . . The collection adds to the knowledge of the (3) . . . involved in second language learning. It points to other dimensions (4) . . . in the development of learner-centred methods and materials. This book will be (5) . . . both classroom and teacher and researcher.
(*The Linguist*)

1 a) quite a few   b) all sorts of   c) a varied range of
2 a) how they learn   b) their learning process   c) picking up
   languages
3 a) mental skills   b) workings of the mind   c) cognitive
   abilities
4 a) to be taken into account   b) that matter   c) involved
5 a) a great help to   b) of interest and practical value
   to   c) just the answer for

TASK SHEET B In each of the passages below, choose the expression you consider most likely to have been used in the original text. The alternatives are given at the end of each passage.

1 But in this (1) . . . city of the Taj, there's more than the Taj to (2) . . .. Agra has other splendours to offer. The massive red sandstone Agra Fort. Once (3) . . . bygone battles and numerous court intrigues, this majestic citadel was the (4) . . . centre of the Mughal dynasty. Within its walls, Hindu and Muslim architecture merge (5) . . .. Like a pearl in a flamboyant sandstone setting, the Moti Masjid (the largest marble mosque in the world) (6) . . . the prayer call of the muezzin. It is (7) . . . reminder of Mughal religious fervour.
(*A Guide to Agra*)

1 a) fabled   b) (no word)   c) ancient
2 a) be considered   b) attract one's attention   c) feast your eyes on
3 a) the site of   b) mute witness to   c) riven by
4 a) power   b) flourishing   c) (no word)   d) acknowledged
5 a) harmoniously   b) in an elegant structural and decorative whole   c) to create awesome splendour
6 a) echoes to this day to   b) still preserves   b) continues to give voice to
7 a) a timeless   b) an eloquent   c) an evocative   d) a fitting

2 She was indeed an extraordinary writer and had a completely (1) . . . voice. Jean Rhy's strange and (2) . . . novels distil the alienation and (3) . . . of women who have – somehow – slipped a little. Here, from the early days on Dominica, to gin-and-bedsitter life in England, to Paris with her first husband, she gives us a rich, funny, as well as (4) . . . autobiography of her early life.
(back-cover blurb for *Smile Please*)

1 a) consistent   b) intelligible   c) original
2 a) haunting   b) well-researched   c) instructive
3 a) castigation   b) despair   c) non-acceptance
4 a) comprehensive   b) studious   c) moving   d) painstaking

KEY TO TASKS Original wording of the passages:

Task sheet A
1 1b),   2c),   3a),   4b)
2 1c),   2b),   3c),   4a),   5b)

Task sheet B
1 1a),   2c),   3b),   4b),   5c),   6a),   7b)
2 1c),   2a),   3b),   4c)

5.4 Colloquialisms

1 The tasks in this activity could be spread over two lessons, the first dealing with colloquial idioms (step 1a), and the second with proverbs and popular sayings (step 1b).

a. Select passages containing colloquial idioms/phrasal verbs. You will find examples of these in task sheets A and B.

b. Try to find passages incorporating proverbs and popular sayings. Examples are given in task sheets C and D. The tasks in steps 1a and 1b do not, of course, fall into separate categories. The grouping is one of convenience.

2 Make up enough task sheets for everyone in the class.

1 As a warm-up activity, arrange the students in groups of five or six (or, if the class is small, ask them to work as a single group).

2 Write up or call out eight to ten key words in English, for instance:

– *water*	– *time*
– *fire*	– *heart*
– *gold*	– *hand*
– *iron*	– *eye*
– *lion*	– *dog*
etc.	

The students should write down any colloquial idioms or proverbs associated with these words, for instance:

- *There's no smoke without fire*
- *Out of the frying pan into the fire*
- *Strike while the iron's hot*
- *the lion's share*
- *a dog's life*
  etc.

After five minutes, the students should pool and discuss their suggestions.

This task can be extended by asking the students to give any idiomatic associations with the same words in their mother tongue.

3 Hand out the task sheets and get the students to work in groups of three to discuss the examples in the task sheets and decide in each case how they could best render the expressions in italics. They then compare and discuss their versions.

4 (Optional) Extend the discussion of proverbs and sayings by introducing any which were not mentioned in step 1. (Some suggestions are given in task sheet E.)

1 While idiomatic expressions abound in English, proverbs are used quite sparingly. The purpose of the activity, then, is not so much to teach proverbs as to help the students develop tactics for dealing with proverbs (or fragments of proverbs) when they occur in a text. With the colloquial expressions, the main point of discussion will be: what approaches can be used if no suitable idiom exists in L1 (for example, for *teething problems*, *uphill struggle*, *keep the company afloat*)?

Idiomatic expressions are notoriously difficult to translate. As a general rule, I would suggest to you and to the students that if a suitable idiom in your own language does not readily spring to mind, you give a straightforward translation of the meaning (*teething problems* = initial difficulties). Other rules of thumb would be:

a. Do not translate an idiomatic expression literally if it makes no sense in your own language, for example: the Serbian expression *pod gasom* (drunk, tipsy) cannot be rendered literally in English as *under gas* or *under the accelerator*.

b. Ask yourself if the idiomatic expression is 'dead' or 'alive' – a cliché, or a vivid image. An *uphill struggle*, for instance, is a fairly routine image in English. Roughly equivalent to *une lutte acharnée* in French. With such fixed expressions, there is no need to search for 'colourful' solutions.

c. If the image is powerful, or strikingly concise, such as the celebrated *glasnost*, retain the original word with an approximation in brackets ('openness').

2 This activity is complementary to many activities in section 1.

TASK SHEET A

In the passages below, the expressions in italics are colloquial, that is, more common in everyday speech than in formal writing.

Before translating, discuss what you think is the literal meaning of each expression (for example, *get hold of the wrong end of the stick* –to misunderstand what is meant). Then translate the passages orally, noting down the suggestions for each expression in italics.

1 **Health and Efficiency – A Plan by Jordans**

On busy days when you really have to *put your back into it*, don't *turn your back on your body*. Our original Crunchy Bars are high in fibre, making digestion faster, more efficient.
(advertisement for Jordans chocolate)

2 If you are a student and I am your teacher, *it's up to you* to let me know if my input is unclear. If you haven't understood, tell me.

Study conditions can sometimes be difficult for you as well. *If I get hold of the wrong end of the stick* because I don't know what the problem is, I can't help you. If you tell me what's wrong, then *it's my job* to help you sort it out.
(informal briefing to new students)

3 People come to Bombay *to 'make it'*, not to idle. Consequently there are thousands in marginal occupations.
(Trevor Fishlock: *India File*)

4 But does all this mean that the general public should not be more scientifically educated? On the contrary! All it means is that scientific education for the masses will do little good, and probably a lot of harm, if *it simply boils down to* more physics, more chemistry, more biology, etc., to the detriment of literature and history.
(George Orwell: *Collected Essays*)

5 The recent rise in interest rates has meant that many couples are *facing an uphill struggle* to keep up their monthly mortgage repayments. Buyers who acquired property needing modernization, and who may have spent large sums on improvements have been particularly hard hit just when they thought their *teething problems had been sorted out*.
(*Property Review*)

TASK SHEET B

In the passages below, the expressions in italics are colloquial, that is, more common in everyday speech than in formal writing.

Before translating, discuss what you think is the literal meaning of each expression (for example, *know the ropes* – be experienced in the job, know what is to be done). Then translate the passages orally, noting down the suggestions for each expression in italics.

1 I had a difficult time making a living out of writing at the start, though looking back now, and knowing *what a racket* literary journalism is, I see that I could have managed much better *if I had known the ropes*.
(George Orwell: *Collected Essays*)

2 I'M BACKING BRITAIN – but *backing Britain* into what?
(sticker on the rear window of a car)

3 The problem of determining the constancy of the IQ is a very complex one, but *ultimately it boils down to* a simple comparison of the IQ achieved by a child at one age, and the IQ achieved by the same child at a later age.
(H. J. Eysenck: *Check Your Own IQ*)

4 (In the Nottinghamshire coal-mining community) the woman almost invariably nagged about material things. She was taught to do it; she was encouraged to do it. It was a mother's business to see that her sons '*got on*', and it was the man's business to provide the money.
(D. H. Lawrence, autobiographical sketch)

5 'Bernard,' I said firmly, 'this government governs. It does not just preside like our predecessors did. When a nation's been *going downhill*^(*) you need someone to get into the driving seat and put his foot on the accelerator.' 'I think, perhaps, you mean the brake, Minister,' said Bernard.
(Jonathan Lynn and Anthony Jay: *Yes, Minister*)

TASK SHEET C

The following passages contain proverbs and popular sayings. Try to find suitable equivalents in your own language for the expressions in italics in the passages below. In many cases, a literal translation will not be possible. Feel free, then, to experiment, but try to suit your translation to the context of the passage.

1 The teacher can suggest the best distribution of time for adequate training. Should learning periods be long? Should we '*strike while the iron is hot*', or should we do a little at a time and avoid fatigue? The optimum length for the learning periods will vary from task to task and the teacher should be able to advise. In general it is found that short periods with appreciable rest periods between are most economical.
(C. J. Adcock: *Fundamentals of Psychology*)

2 PRACTICE REALLY DOES MAKE PERFECT

Without doubt, Chris Evert has secured her place in the Tennis Hall of Fame. On court, Chris Evert is a very tough competitor indeed. Off court, however, she reveals both wit and charm. These two contrasting facets of Chris Evert – machine-like efficiency, and feminine charm and style – are also perfectly embodied in her watch. 'I know that Rolex have been making watches for a long time, and "*practice makes perfect*" is something I agree with.'
(advertisement for Rolex watches)

3 The *moral fibre* which sustained mid-Victorian Britain in its era of greatness was derived only partly from the values of liberalism. The evils of philistinism, smugness, and bad taste were there from the first: it was when they ceased to be restrained and offset by the practice of the Christian virtues that *the moral rot set in*.
(David Thomson: *England in the Nineteenth Century*)

4 THE CUP – *BY THE SKIN OF THEIR TEETH!*
Coventry clinch it: Coventry City 3   Tottenham Hotspur 2

5 The latest Fire Test Certification tests on Pilkington Glass demonstrate yet again its ability to hold back flames and smoke for at least 60 minutes. *Don't play with fire.* Specify Pilkington Polished Wired Glass, *and you'll be on the safe side*.
(advertisement for Pilkington Glass)

TASK SHEET D

The following passages contain proverbs and popular sayings. Try to find suitable equivalents in your own language for the expressions in italics in the passages below. In many cases, a literal translation will not be possible. Feel free, then, to experiment, but try to suit your translation to the context of the passage.

1 Common opinion tends to stress the importance of practice. We say: '*Practice makes perfect*', but this is certainly not true. In an experiment with dart throwing, subjects were given long continued practice, but each time they threw a dart the light was switched off before they could see the result. Under these circumstances their scores deteriorated rather than improved. The value of practice is that it enables us to discover what works. But unless we know the results of our effort there can be no reward and so no reinforcement.
(C. J. Adcock: *Fundamentals of Psychology*)

2 THE ROT. AND HOW TO STOP IT
Wet rot, dry rot, and woodworm. Three little things *hellbent on* destroying the wood in your home. With 5-Star Cuprinol there's no need to worry about what sort of rot you've got because *it gets rid of the lot*. Cuprinol 5 Star. There's no better way *to stop the rot*.
(advertisement for Cuprinol wood-preserver)

3 A third cause of disagreement between IQ measures and external criteria may be related to motivation. If *we can lead a horse to the water*, so we can send a child to school, but as we *cannot make the horse drink*, so we cannot make the child learn unless he is in fact motivated.
(H. J. Eysenck: *Check Your Own IQ*)

4 THERE COMES A TIME WHEN *SILENCE ISN'T GOLDEN*
Whether it's a telephone that doesn't ring, or a cherished instrument that sits silently in a corner, *the twilight years* of a musician can prove deathly quiet. After a life where the sound of applause was an everyday event, the *silence can prove deafening*. But you can help.
(appeal for the Musicians Benevolent Fund)

"There comes a time when silence isn't golden."

Whether it's a telephone that doesn't ring, or a cherished instrument that sits silently in a corner, the twilight years of a musician can prove deathly quiet.

After a life where the sound of applause was an everyday event, the silence can prove deafening.

But you can help.

A donation to the Musicians Benevolent Fund could well become music to their ears.

Even better remember the Fund in your Will. That way your love of music can live on for others to enjoy.

PLEASE SEND A DONATION, LARGE OR SMALL, TO:

MUSICIANS BENEVOLENT FUND

SIR IAN HUNTER, CHAIRMAN,

16 OGLE STREET, LONDON W1P 7LG.

Idiomatic expressions cannot, in the proper sense, be defined. If they could, they would probably not be idiomatic. These notes are not intended as definitions, but merely as a guide to the literal meaning of some of the less obvious expressions in the exercises.

When translating, remember that word play in one language cannot often be properly conveyed in another. Aim to be natural rather than clever. Translate the meaning rather than the words.

Task sheet A

1 *put your back into it:* make a great effort
turn your back on: ignore, forget about

2 *it's up to you:* it is your responsibility
If I get hold of the wrong end of the stick: If I do not properly understand the conditions
it's my job: my responsibility

3 *to 'make it':* succeed, make money

4 *it boils down to:* it means, involves, results in

5 *an uphill struggle:* a hard battle, a difficult task
teething problems: early, usually minor, difficulties (Children tend to cry when their first teeth come through – this is 'teething'.)

Task sheet B

1 *a racket:* a profitable, but not very honest profession
if I had known the ropes: if I had known the 'rules of the game', the 'tricks of the trade', that is, how to do the job best and most easily.

2 *I'm backing Britain:* play on words – backing = supporting, and also reversing (going backwards)

3 *it boils down to:* it means, involves, results in

4 *'got on':* succeeded, made money, and advanced socially

5 *going downhill:* deteriorating, getting worse

Task sheet C

1 *'strike while the iron is hot'* – proverb. If you feel like getting something done, do it now; always act when you feel motivated and when the conditions are right.

2 *'Practice makes perfect':* a proverb, meaning that true skill in any work comes from hard training

3 *moral fibre:* strength of character, honesty, decency, reliability (the great Victorian virtues)
moral rot: decadence, the undermining of moral values
the . . . rot set in: a popular expression meaning things started to deteriorate, people lost their moral strength, or, generally, a decline began.

4 *by the skin of their teeth:* popular expression – by a narrow margin, very closely, only just

5 *Don't play with fire* (if you don't want to get your fingers burnt):

popular saying meaning do not take dangerous risks if you do not want to be hurt.

on the safe side: common expression for not taking risks, being cautious and wise. Here the words are deliberately used in the literal sense as well, that is, you will be 'on the safe side' of the door.

Task sheet D

1 *'Practice makes perfect':* a proverb, meaning that true skill in any work comes from hard training

2 *hellbent on destroying:* colloquial – determined to destroy
   stop the rot: colloquial expression meaning put an end to bad practices, bad behaviour, bad attitudes, etc.

3 *lead a horse to the water* . . . The full proverb is: 'You can lead a horse to the water, but you can't make him drink'. You can show people what they need or what they should do, but you cannot make them do it.

4 *a time when silence isn't golden:* an inversion of the saying 'silence is golden', meaning it is good or wise to be quiet; silence is precious
   the twilight years: old age
   silence can prove deafening: the popular expression is 'a deafening silence' – an unexpected, shocking silence

---

TASK SHEET E

Below are some familiar proverbs and popular sayings. Mark any for which an equivalent – close or rough – exists in your own language. For the others, suggest a possible translation, literal or free.

1   1 Absence makes the heart grow fonder.
    2 Out of sight, out of mind.
    3 It is better to travel hopefully than to arrive.
    4 Travel broadens the mind.
    5 The grass is always greener on the other side of the fence.
    6 East, West, home's best.

2   1 Look before you leap.
    2 He who hesitates is lost.
    3 Don't cross your bridges before you come to them.
    4 Strike while the iron is hot.
    5 Discretion is the better part of valour.

3   1 Practice makes perfect.
    2 Practise what you preach.
    3 Great minds think alike.
    4 Fools never differ.
    5 There's many a true word spoken in jest.
    6 He who laughs last laughs longest.

4 1 The early bird catches the worm.
2 Birds of a feather flock together.
3 When the cat's away the mice will play.
4 Let sleeping dogs lie.
5 You can lead a horse to water but you can't make him drink.
6 The leopard cannot change his spots.
7 Talk of the Devil and he's sure to appear.

5 1 Too many cooks spoil the broth.
2 Many hands make light work.
3 You can't burn the candle at both ends.
4 A bad workman blames his tools.
5 One man's meat is another man's poison.

6 1 Two's company, three's a crowd.
2 Beauty is in the eye of the beholder.
3 No news is good news.
4 There's no smoke without fire.
5 Out of the frying-pan, into the fire.

5.5 Variations on a theme: reformulations

PREPARATION

1 Choose a text of medium length (ten to fifteen lines). Present it in three different versions, one of which is the original. (For suggestions on ways of obtaining such material, see *Comments*.)

This activity is designed as a written exercise, to be done out of class. The writing will then be used later for class discussion.

2 Prepare a task sheet and make enough copies for the whole class. Examples of the type of material are given in task sheets A and B.

3 Give each student a task sheet to work on out of class.

IN CLASS

1 Divide the students into three groups, according to which text they have translated. (If one of the groups is too large, it can be divided.) Allow ten to fifteen minutes for comparison of translations and discussion of difficulties.

2 Ask the students to work in pairs, each with a partner who has translated a different version of the text. They then compare translations, concentrating on the main points of difference.

COMMENTS

1 In this activity, we are following the three essential stages of translation:

a. forming thoughts (in the SL)
b. finding the suitable expression (context/register, SL and L1)
c. recreating the text in another language.

The point of the activity is not to spot the original text, but to spot the differences between the three versions.

2 Practical problems:

a. Finding suitable texts may be difficult. Useful material can be found in, for instance: draft reports and final versions; different newspaper accounts of the same event; references to printed documents made in interviews; and, particularly for literature students, revisions by writers to their works.

b. What if the students nearly all choose the same text? This could easily happen. The most obvious solution is to give the students only one passage each for translation. They then meet in groups of three (*In class*, step 2 is left out), and compare texts. In this way, there will be no problems of grouping.

But I still believe it is more interesting to leave the choice of text to the student, because this will give added commitment to the translation.

TASK SHEET A

Read through these three passages. One of them is the original text, the other two are reformulations based on the original. Decide which text you think is the original, and translate it as accurately as possible. The other texts may help to make certain points clearer, but they must not be brought into your translation.

a) One of the most important points about this new office block is that it makes use of an effective heat recovery system which maintains office temperatures at 21°C. The basic principle of the system is that it uses reclaimed heat which has been generated within the building from lights, office machinery, and occupants. In this way, a controlled even temperature within offices can be achieved for a relatively small increase in capital outlay, at the same time cutting down energy consumption to a minimum.

b) A vital feature of this new office block is its superbly functional heat-recovery system, which keeps the office temperature at a steady 21°C. Basically, this is how the system works: it takes in all the heat given out by people, lights, machines, etc. and re-uses it. Which means you can have a controlled, constant temperature in all the offices by investing just a little more at first. And at the same time, you'll be slashing your fuel bill!

c) Notable features of the heat-recovery system of this new office block include the following:
    1 effective maintenance of office temperature, at 21°C
    2 a system based on the principle of energy-recovery: heat generated in the building (by lights, machines, occupants) is reclaimed and re-used
    3 regulated temperature-levels in offices, at relatively little additional cost
    4 reduction of energy consumption to the minimum.

TASK SHEET B   Read through these three passages. One of them is the original text, the other two are reformulations based on the original. Decide which text you think is the original, and translate it as accurately as possible. The other texts may help to make certain points clearer, but they must not be brought into your translation.

a) **Dr Marsh** When one is 'day-dreaming', as the expression goes, one can imagine oneself as being exceptionally strong or ourstandingly gifted. One could marry a prince or come into a fortune. And the only limit is our own imagination. Our plans, in these day-dreams, don't have to be ones that would ·actually work in practice, because we can *imagine* getting what we want, and how to get it! Daydreaming offers such wonderful solutions to our problems that some people who can't face up to the ordinary demands of life end up relying completely on their dreams. Unforuntately, though this may satisfy them *mentally*, it doesn't satisfy them physically. And so they may end up needing institutional care.

b) *Daydreaming* Popular expression for the indulgence in fancy or reverie while awake. In this condition, the subject may imagine himself endowed with exceptional capacities, e.g. unusual strength or remarkable skills. This may be accompanied by illusions such as marrying a prince or inheriting a fortune. The only limitation to daydreaming is that of the individual's own imaginative powers. In this condition, the imaginary plans of action need not be those which could be practically realized, since both the achievement of the (imagined) goal and the means by which it is attained are products of the imagimation.

One of the consequences of daydreaming is that, because it offers a potential solution to personal problems, it may become an indispensable defence-mechanism for persons unable to deal with the practical demands of life. The regrettable consequence of this is that daydreaming, while satisfying the needs of the mind, fails to satisfy those of the body. As a result, daydreamers may eventually require therapeutic treatment.

c) In the process of what we usually call 'day-dreaming' we can imagine ourselves with unusual strength or unexpected abilities. We can marry a prince or inherit a fortune. We are limited only by our own imaginations. Our plan of action does not have to be the one which is likely to succeed in practice because we are able to imagine the achievement of our goal as well as the means to its achievement. There are such wonderful possibilities in this solution of our problems that some people, unable to cope with the practical requirements of life, fall back completely on it. Unfortunately it fails to give physiological satisfaction with its psychological satisfaction, so that such people may require institutional care.

KEY TO TASKS

The original passages are:

Task sheet A
a) from an article in *The Architects' Journal*

Task sheet B
c) from C. J. Adcock: *Fundamentals of Psychology*

5.6 Variations on a theme: reverse translation

PREPARATION

1 Choose two passages of ten to fifteen lines, one in English and one in the mother tongue. The texts should preferably be self-contained, that is, easy to understand even out of context.

Two specimen examples, 'Code and Metaphor' and 'L' Hôpital Général' are given in task sheets A and B.

2 Prepare a task sheet for each passage and make copies for half the class.

IN CLASS

1 Divide the class into two even groups, A and B. Give Group A task sheet A, Group B, task sheet B. Out of class, the students translate their respective texts. Group A from English to L1, Group B from L1 into English.

2 Each student chooses a partner from the opposite group. They exchange translations but not original texts. Their task is to translate the translation they have been given, either back into English (Group B) or back into L1 (Group A).

The students should do the reverse translation alone, without discussion or consultation. It could even be done out of class, but interest will be greater if the writing is done on the spot. A strict time-limit of 20 minutes should be set.

3 Next, ask each student to rejoin his or her partner, and:

a. Discuss any difficulties they have had. They should refer only to the translations, not to the original text.
b. Read through each other's work.
c. Exchange the original texts and compare them with the reverse translation.

COMMENTS

1 The activity can succeed only if the students are mature enough to 'play the game' and not show each other their texts out of class.

Task sheet B is an example of the kind of L1 text that you might use. It is given with the original English translation (which could be used as a further point of contrast in discussion).

2 The great value of this activity is that it shows clearly how errors can creep into translation. It also provides a basis for discussing how such errors can be avoided.

3 Since it is nearly always easier to translate <u>into</u> the mother tongue, it is important that the English text (in task sheet A) should not be too difficult. (This is the passage Group B will have to translate back into English, in class.)

4 For this activity, I am indebted to Alan Maley and Mario Rinvolucri, both of whom independently suggested the same idea.

TASK SHEET A

Translate the text below into your own language.

Code and Metaphor

A simple example of what I shall call a visual metaphor is the use of the colour red in certain cultural contexts. Red, being the colour of flames and of blood, offers itself as a metaphor for anything that is strident or violent. It is no accident, therefore, that it was selected as the code sign for 'stop' in our traffic code and as a label of revolutionary parties in politics.

But though both these applications are grounded on simple biological facts, the colour red itself has no fixed 'meaning'. A future historian or anthropologist, for instance, who wanted to interpret the significance of the label 'red' in politics would get no guidance from his knowledge of our traffic code. Should the colour that denotes 'stop' not stand for the 'conservatives' and green for the 'go-ahead' progressives? And how should he interpret the meaning of the red hat of the cardinal or the Red Cross?

(E. H. Gombrich, 'Visual Metaphors of Value in Art', in *Meditations on a Hobby Horse*).

TASK SHEET B

Translate the passage below into English.

L'Hôpital Général, lieu d'enfermement

Si au XVIIe siècle on assiste à une prise de conscience d'une partie de la haute société des misères du temps, paradoxalement l'hôpital devient lieu d'enfermement des déshérités, 'des marginaux': le mendiant, l'infirme, le malade, le vieillard, le paysan dépossédé de ses terres, le soldat sans guerre, l'enfant abandonné.

Dans cette salle est exposé dans une vitrine un édit de Louis XIV du 27 avril 1656 créant l'Hôpital Général où seront enfermés les pauvres. L'Hôpital Général va regrouper plusieurs maisons dont la plus connue est la Salpétrière, que l'on peut voir sur plusieurs gravures.

A coté de portraits de personnages qui furent à la direction de l'Hôpital Général, des affiches, documents authentiques ou reproductions, indiquent qu'en plus des dons et des revenus de son patrimoine, l'Hôpital Général tirait ses ressources d'un droit sur les cartes a jouer, d'une taxe sur les spectacles et d'une loterie.

('Le Musée de l'assistance publique des hôpitaux de Paris', in Air France: *Atlas*, April 1987)

The General Hospital, a place of confinement

In the XVIIth century, a part of aristocratic society became conscious of the miseries that people suffered at that time. But paradoxically hospitals became places of confinement for the needy and the 'marginal': beggars, the infirm, the sick, the old, peasants dispossessed of their land, soldiers with no wars to fight, abandoned children.

In a cabinet in this room is an Edict of Louis XIV of April 27th 1656 establishing the General Hospital, in which destitute people were to be confined. The General Hospital was to include several homes, of which the best known is la Salpétrière; it is to be seen here on several engravings.

Alongside portraits of dignitaries who presided over the General Hospital there are posters, both originals and reproductions, which reveal that it derived revenue not only from donations and investment income but also from a duty on playing cards, a tax on public entertainments and a lottery.

(Air France: *Atlas*)

5.7 Spoken language, written language: voices of the past

PREPARATION

1 This activity provides examples of writing from earlier centuries, including quotations to be found in modern works. You may wish to use similar passages of your own choice.

2 Make enough copies of one of the task sheets for the whole class.

IN CLASS

1 Give all the students a task sheet and ask them to translate the passage(s) out of class, in a style appropriate to the period.

2 In class, in groups of four or five, the students compare translations.

Follow this up with a general class discussion focusing on any particular difficulties.

COMMENTS

Although students will not often have to reproduce language of the past, they do need to recognize it in their reading (both L1 and SL).

The activity may not be relevant to the needs of the general language student. But I have included it because it touches on a matter that is rarely discussed, and yet is of importance to students of literature and to all translators.

TASK SHEET A

The passages below were written or contain material written before the twentieth century. In text 2, where the material is quoted in a modern work, part of the surrounding text is given.

In translating the passage or quotation, try to find an appropriate idiom in your own language to capture the flavour of the past.

1 After we came out of the church, we stood talking for some time together of Bishop Berkeley's ingenious sophistry to prove the non-existence of matter, and that everything in the universe is merely ideal. I observed, that though we are satisfied his doctrine is not true, it is impossible to refute it. I shall never forget the alacrity with which Johnson answered, striking his foot with mighty force against a large stone, till he rebounded from it. 'I refute it thus!'

(James Boswell: *Life of Johnson,* circa 1710)

2 A small group of Englishmen conceived the idea of seeking a north-eastern passage to Asia through Arctic waters. As early as 1527 a small book had appeared prophesying such a discovery. One phrase rings out: 'There is no land uninhabitable, nor sea unnavigable.'

(quoted in Winston Churchill: *A History of the English Speaking Peoples*)

NOTE: You may make photocopies of this for classroom use (but please note that copyright law does not normally permit multiple copying of published material).

TASK SHEET B

The passage quoted below was written in the eighteenth century. In translating the passage, try to find an appropriate idiom in your own language to capture the flavour of the past.

(The writer has travelled to the Pacific island of Selkirk to see the place where Robinson Crusoe had lived. *The Life and Strange*

Surprising Adventures of Robinson Crusoe of York, Mariner, 'a fiction
from the mind of Daniel Defoe, was based on the almost equally
surprising adventures of Alexander Selkirk, first mate of the 120-
ton privateer 'Cinque Ports' who after a dispute with the master
refused to sail on with him from Cumberland Bay in October 1704.'
The passage below is a quotation from Sir Richard Steele's
encounter, in 1713, with the original Robinson Crusoe, Alexander
Selkirk):

> When I first saw him, I thought, if I had not been let into his
> Character and Story, I could have discerned that he had been
> much separated from Company, from his Aspect and Gesture;
> there was a strong but cheerful seriousness in his Look, and a
> certain Disregard to the ordinary things about him, as if he had
> been sunk in Thought. When the ship which brought him off the
> Island came in, he received them with the greatest Indifference,
> with relation to the Prospect of going off with them, but with
> great satisfaction in an opportunity to refresh and help them. The
> man frequently bewailed his Return to the World, which could
> not, he said, with all its Enjoyments, restore him to the
> Tranquility of his Solitude.

(quoted in Gavin Young: *Slow Boats Home*)

TASK SHEET C   Translate the passage below, paying particular attention to the
vocabulary and tone of the text.

The Elephant

The Elephant (which some call an oliphant) is the biggest of all
fourfooted beasts, his forelegs are longer than his hinder, he hath
ankles in the lower part of his hinder legs, and five toes on his feet
undivided, his snout or trunk is so long, and in such form, that it is
to him in the stead of a hand: for he neither eateth nor drinketh but
by bringing his trunk to his mouth, therewith he helpeth up his
master or keeper, therewith he overthroweth trees. Of all beasts
they are most gentle and tractable, and are of quick sense and
sharpness of wit. They love rivers, and will often go into them up to
the snout, wherewith they blow and snuff and play in the water.
They have continual war against dragons, which desire their blood
because it is very cold: and therefore the dragon lieth in wait as the
elephant passeth by.

(Richard Hakluyt: *Voyages and Discoveries*, 1554)

5.8 Spoken language, written language: speech in writing

Transcripts of interviews, radio broadcasts, debates, and discussions are particularly suitable for this activity. Film and play scripts could also be used. This is primarily an oral activity, though some writing will be involved.

PREPARATION

1 Take the transcript of an interview or radio talk (see task sheet) and divide it into five to ten roughly equal sections.

2 Make up enough task sheets for the whole class.

IN CLASS

1 Ask the students to work in groups of three, and give each student the complete text. The groups should, however, work on only one or two sections of the passage.

2 Tell the students to imagine that they have been asked by the editor of the local newspaper to translate the talk or interview. They should first read through the whole passage. Then, in their groups, they discuss how they would translate the expressions in italics. Ask them to note down all their suggestions.

3 Next, each group compares ideas with others who have worked on the same sections of the text.

4 Conduct a class discussion with all the groups together. Find out from the students which expressions gave them the most difficulty and how the expressions could best be translated.

COMMENTS

1 It is common practice, in most countries, to 'borrow' talks and interviews for broadcasting or publication. This is therefore a real, not invented, task for the translator. To remind the students that what they are doing is common practice, bring to class a few copies of local newspapers or magazines and point out any translated articles or interviews. Also, keep an eye open for any radio or TV programmes which will involve the translation of speech.

2 For further ideas and more material, see activity 5.9. The passage in the task sheet is intended as a bridge between this activity and activity 5.9, and could be translated either as suggested here or in the form of subtitles (no more than four to each numbered section of the text).

TASK SHEET

The text opposite is taken from the transcript of a television interview with the spy-story writer, Len Deighton. You have been asked to translate this for the Arts Review section of one of your major Sunday newspapers. The text is complete, but you need translate only one or two sections.

1 **Melvyn Bragg** (interviewer) Len Deighton is a Londoner, and
in true Dickensian fashion, by a series of accidents, he was born
in a workhouse. But he was brought up in a very grand London
square, Montagu Square. Well, not exactly in the square –
behind the square, in the mews, because his parents worked at
the great house.

2 His life continued to follow a rather Dickensian fashion – he
went from job to job, all different, and all just keeping him
going, until he landed up an international best-selling writer.

3 He now lives part of the time in Portugal, and it was there that I
went to talk to him. We began with his first novel, *The Ipcress
File*.

4 **Len Deighton** I went on holiday, and I decided I would write a
story. Most people who come to writing books have an
experience of writing words before, and they know certain facts
about writing which I didn't know. For instance, they know
that a book tends to be between 70,000 and 100,000 words long

5 and they have a very good idea of how many words that is. For
all I knew, you sat down and wrote a book and by the weekend
it was ready. So when I say to you that I started out to write *The
Ipcress File* as a story, I had no idea whether it would be

6 a short story, or a long story, or a book. When I was halfway
through it, I put it aside, and when I went on holiday again the
next year I wrote the rest of it. And then I came back to London
– I was still doing drawings for a living – and I put it in a drawer.

7 Then I met a man at a party, a literary agent, and he said: 'Why
don't you let me have it?' And then eventually, after being
turned down at a couple of places, he found a publisher who was
prepared to publish it. But I didn't do it with a view to taking it
to a publisher and getting it published.

8 **Melvyn Bragg** Yet it subsequently went on to sell about two
million copies.
Len Deighton It was no part of a plan of mine – in fact, I had
never read a James Bond book – but by an extraordinary
coincidence, the month that *The Ipcress File* was published was
the month that the first James Bond film appeared in the West
End.

9 One of my friends came up to me and said: 'You're very lucky,
Len, because you're a blunt instrument that the critics used to
smash Ian Fleming (author of the James Bond stories) over the
head with.' And this is really, I think, true, that a lot of people
who perhaps liked the film

10 but didn't like the sort of success the film was having, were
over-generous to me when I came along with something which
was a substantially different thing from the James Bond books.
(BBC2 television; text reproduced in *The Listener*)

5.9 Spoken language, written language: translation and adaptation; subtitles and synchronization

Extracts from plays or films, dialogue passages from novels, the texts of documentary films, and extracts from travel books provide the most suitable material for this activity.

The text can be presented either as a complete sequence or in the form of short passages, each corresponding to a limited number of subtitles (as in the example material in task sheet A).

PREPARATION

1 When you have chosen your text, prepare a task sheet.

2 Make enough copies for the whole class.

IN CLASS

1 First check that the students understand fully what is meant by subtitles or by synchronization. It is essential that they accept the constraints, particularly of time and length, as real ones. To meet these constraints, the text will almost certainly have to be cut or condensed.

2 Ask the students to work in pairs, each with two or three consecutive passages for subtitling. (Preferably, each pair should be given the complete text, with their particular passages marked.)

3 Set a time-limit of approximately ten minutes for them to decide on their subtitles and translate them. Each pair then compares subtitles with others who have worked on the same passages. They then move on to the next two passages in the sequence.

4 Follow up with a general discussion focusing on what details had to be left out and why.

VARIATION

An alternative approach is to give the students the full text and ask them to work on it on their own, out of class.

COMMENTS

1 This is what might be called 'applied translation', or translation for specific purposes. For the activity to succeed, it is essential that the students believe in what they are doing. The words they write down are the words which will appear on the television screen, or be spoken by the actors.

One way of making the activity more realistic would be to ask the local television station to let you have the scripts of English-language films due to be shown with subtitles or voice-overs.

2 One of the problems which this activity throws into relief is that of dealing with cultural references and associations, such as *the Old Edwardian brigade, croquet, Vaughan Williams*, which may mean little in translation (if they <u>can</u> be translated). Subtitling allows for some of these references to be left out. But if they are left out, the students should know why – and this should come up in the discussion.

TASK SHEET A   Your local television station has sent you the text below for
translation into subtitles. It is from a documentary series called
Modern Explorers. The text is complete, but it has been divided up
to show where the subtitles are required. Translate each section,
using one or at the most two subtitles. The maximum length for a
subtitle is two lines, and the limit for each line is 40 spaces. A space
is a letter or punctuation mark, or a gap between words.

Easter Island

1 Easter Island is the loneliest inhabited place in the world. The
   nearest solid land the inhabitants can see is in the firmament,
   the moon and the planets.

2 They have to travel farther than any other people to see that
   there really is land still closer. Therefore they live nearest to the
   stars and know more names of stars than of towns and countries
   in our own world.

3 On this remote island, east of the sun and west of the moon,
   mankind once had one of its most curious ideas. No one knows
   who had it, and no one knows why.

4 For it happened before Columbus went to America, and in so
   doing opened the gate for voyages of exploration out into the
   great unknown Pacific.

5 While Europeans still believed that the world ended at Gibraltar
   there were other great navigators who knew better. In advance
   of their time they ploughed unknown seas in the immense
   watery void off the desolate west coast of South America.

6 Far out they found land. The loneliest little island in the world.

7 They landed there, whetted their stone adzes and set about one
   of the most remarkable engineering projects of ancient times.

8 They did not build fortresses and castles, or dams and wharves.
   They made gigantic stone figures in man's likeness,

9 as tall as houses and as heavy as railway trucks; they dragged
   them in great numbers across country and set them up erect on
   huge stone terraces all over the island.

10 How did they manage this, before the mechanical age? No one
   knows. But there stood the figures they had desired, towering
   into the sky, while the people fell.

11 They buried their dead at the feet of the colossi they themselves
   had created. They raised great statues and buried their dead.

12 Then one day the blows of the adze on the rock face fell silent.
   They fell silent suddenly, for the tools were left lying

13 and many of the figures were only half finished. The mysterious
   sculptors disappeared into the dark mists of antiquity.

14 What happened? Yes, what had happened on Easter Island?
   (Thor Heyerdahl: *Aku-Aku*)

TASK SHEET B

The two passages below are taken from John Osborne's play *Look Back in Anger*. In the first, Jimmy is talking to Cliff, who shares the apartment with Jimmy and his wife, Alison; '*her Daddy*' is Alison's father. In the second passage, Alison is talking to her father. In the opening line – 'And what does *he* say about me?' – *he* refers to Jimmy.

You have been asked to translate the texts for a filmed version of the play. Your translation will be used for synchronization, or voice-over. It should therefore be very close in length to the English.

In both passages, there are certain references to English culture and history which may be difficult to translate. There are also certain expressions – some colloquial, some old-fashioned – which will need special attention. (These are all marked in italics.)

The passages are continuous, but they have been broken up to show where the main pauses come. Try to produce a translation which can be easily read aloud and readily understood.

Text 1

1 **Jimmy** Nobody thinks, nobody cares. No beliefs, no convictions and no enthusiasm. Just another Sunday evening. (Cliff sits down)

2 Perhaps there's a concert on. (Picks up Radio Times) Ah. (Nudges Cliff with his foot) Make some more tea. (Cliff grunts. He is reading again.)

3 Oh, yes. There's *a Vaughan Williams*. Well, that's something, anyway. Something strong, something simple, something English. I suppose people like me aren't supposed to be very patriotic.

4 Somebody said – what was it – we get our cooking from Paris (*that's a laugh*), our politics from Moscow, and our morals from Port Said. Something like that, anyway. Who was it? (Pause)

5 Well, you wouldn't know anyway. I hate to admit it, but I think I can understand how her *Daddy* must have felt when he came back from India, after all those years away.

6 *The old Edwardian brigade do make their brief little world look pretty tempting.* All *home-made cakes and croquet, bright ideas,* bright uniforms. Always the same picture: high summer, the long days in the sun, *slim volumes of verse,* crisp linen, the smell of starch.

7 What a romantic picture. *Phoney too,* of course. It must have rained sometimes. Still, even I regret it somehow, *phoney or not.* If you've no world of your own, it's rather pleasant to regret the passing of someone else's.

8 I must be getting sentimental. But I must say it's pretty dreary *living in the American Age* – unless you're an American of course. Perhaps all our children will be Americans. *That's a thought, isn't it?* (He gives Cliff a kick and shouts at him.)

9 Jimmy I said that's a thought!
Cliff You did?
Jimmy You sit there *like a lump of dough*. I thought you were going to make me some tea.
(John Osborne: *Look Back in Anger*)

Text 2

1 Colonel And what does he say about me?
Alison Oh, he doesn't seem to mind you so much. He likes you because he can feel sorry for you. (Conscious that what she says is going to hurt him.)

2 Alison 'Poor old *Daddy* – just one of those sturdy old plants left over from *the Edwardian Wilderness* that can't understand why the sun isn't shining any more'. (Rather lamely) Something like that, anyway.

3 Colonel He has *quite a turn of phrase*, hasn't he? . . . Perhaps Jimmy is right. Perhaps I am a – what was it? an old plant left over from the Edwardian Wilderness. And I can't undertand why the sun isn't shining any more. You can see what he means, can't you?

4 It was March, 1914, when I left England, and, apart from leaves every ten years or so, I didn't see much of my own country until we all came back in '47. Oh, I knew things had changed, of course.

5 People told you all the time the way it was going – *going to the dogs, as the Blimps are supposed to say.* But it seemed very unreal to me out there.

6 The England I remembered was the one I left in 1914, and I was happy to go on remembering it that way. Besides, I had the Maharajah's army to command – that was my world, and I loved it, all of it. All the time, it looked like going on forever.

7 When I think of it now, it seems like a dream. If only it could have gone on forever. Those long cool evenings *up in the hills*, everything purple and golden. Your mother and I were so happy then.

8 It seemed as though we had everything we could ever want. I think the last day the sun shone was when that dirty little train steamed out of that crowded, suffocating Indian station, and the battalion band playing *for all it was worth. I knew in my heart it was all over then.* Everything.

9 Alison You're hurt because everything is changed. Jimmy is hurt because everything is the same. And neither of you can face it. Something's gone wrong somewhere, hasn't it?

(John Osborne: *Look Back in Anger*)

Bibliography

Translation: theory and practice

This list is restricted to books on translation which would be of interest to the language teacher. For a more comprehensive selection, see the bibliography in Peter Newmark: *A Textbook of Translation* (below).

Helmut M. Braem (ed.)   *Übersetzer-Werkstatt.* Munich: Deutscher Taschenbuch Verlag, 1979.

Ágnes Dániel   *A Fordítói Gondolkodás Iskolája.* Budapest: Tankönyvkiadó, 1983.

Alan Duff   *The Third Language.* Oxford: Pergamon Press, 1981.
On recurrent problems of translation into English.

I. Finlay   *Translating.* English Universities Press, 1971.

F. Fuller   *The Translator's Handbook.* The Pennsylvania State University Press, 1984.

G. Mounin   *Les problèmes théoriques de la traduction.* Paris: Gallimard, 1973.

Peter Newmark   *Approaches to Translation.* Oxford: Pergamon Press, 1981.

Peter Newmark   *A Textbook of Translation.* Hemel Hempstead: Prentice Hall International, 1988.
An excellent survey of the essential questions of translation.

George Steiner   *After Babel.* Oxford: Oxford University Press, 1977.

Dr Lóránt Tarnóczi   *Fordítástechnika.* Budapest: OMKDK, 1972.

Wolfram Wilss   *The Science of Translation.* Tübingen: Narr, 1982.

Translation and language learning: textbooks and relevant ELT publications

V. Andrassy, A. Hargreaves, and M. Marušić   *A Workbook for Advanced Students of English.* Zagreb: Sveučilište u Zagrebu (Zagreb University), 1984.

Dennis Chamberlin and Gillian White   *English for Translation* and *Advanced English for Translation.* Cambridge: Cambridge University Press, 1975.

Diana Fried-Booth   *Project Work.* Oxford: Oxford University Press, 1986.
Many useful suggestions which could be adapted to involve use of the mother tongue/translation.

Françoise Grellet,
Alan Maley, and
Wim Welsing

Quartet. Oxford: Oxford University Press, 1983.
Provides valuable practice in the four skills.

Alan Maley and
Alan Duff

Variations on a Theme. Cambridge: Cambridge University Press,
1977.
Listening material, particularly suitable for oral translation.

John Morgan and
Mario Rinvolucri

Vocabulary. Oxford: Oxford University Press, 1986.
Highly relevant to translation work; includes several activities
specially designed for translation.

Sue O'Connell

Focus on Proficiency. London: Collins, 1985.
Ideal language practice material, and a useful source of texts.

Helen Thomas and
Judith Molnár

Hungarian into English and Back. Budapest: International House,
1986.
Excellent translation material and approaches which can be adapted
for use with other languages. (Much of the explanatory text is in
English.)

Catherine Walter

Genuine Articles. Cambridge: Cambridge University Press, 1987.
Particularly suitable for practice in style and register: reading tasks for
students of American English.

On language in general

Richard W Bailey
and Manfred
Görlach

English as a World Language. Cambridge: Cambridge University
Press, 1984.

Wilga M. Rivers

Speaking in Many Tongues. Cambridge: Cambridge University
Press, 1983.

Earl W. Stevick

Teaching and Learning Languages. Cambridge: Cambridge
University Press, 1982.

Louis Trimble

English for Science and Technology. Cambridge: Cambridge
University Press, 1985.

Dictionaries, grammars, and reference works

There are so many good works in this area that I can mention only a
few which would be of particular value to the teacher working with
translation. Of the dictionaries, I would strongly recommend:

The Oxford Advanced Learner's Dictionary of Current English
The Oxford Student's Dictionary of Current English

The Concise Oxford Dictionary
The Collins Dictionary of the English Language
The Collins-Robert French-English / English-French Dictionary
The Collins Bilingual Pocket Dictionaries (Greek, Italian, German, Spanish, French, etc.)
The Longman Learner's Dictionary of English (English-Italian)

But I must stress that this is only a small selection of the best. Of the grammars and reference works, I would suggest:

John Eastwood and Ronald Mackin *A Basic English Grammar*. Oxford: Oxford University Press, 1988. Clear, well laid out, and ideal for use with foreign learners of English.

Tom Huchinson *Using Grammar Books in the Classroom*. Oxford: Oxford University Press, 1987.

Michael Swan *Practical English Usage* and *Basic English Usage*. Oxford: Oxford University Press, 1980 and 1984. Two valuable and lucid guides to some of the commonest errors made by non-native speakers of English.

Articles

For regular articles on translation, see *The Linguist*, Journal of the Institute of Linguists (24a Highbury Grove, London N5 2EA). Below I have given only articles mentioned in this book.

Peter Newmark 'Sixty further propositions on translation'. *The Linguist*, vol. 18 no. 1, 1979.

Dr Ian Tudor 'Using translation in ESP' *ELT Journal* Volume 41/4, October 1987.

Dr Ian Tudor 'A framework for the translational analysis of texts'. *The Linguist*, spring 1987.

A. G. Weymouth 'A learner-centred approach to translation at the post "A" level stage.' *The Linguist*, summer 1984.